Awakening the Guru Within

A practical guide to finding your purpose and destiny

Joyce Fennell

Copyright © 2018 Joyce Fennell.

All rights reserved. This book or any portion thereof may not be reproduced or used in any manner whatsoever without the express written permission of the publisher, except for the use of brief quotations in a book review.

All artwork created by Joyce Fennell.

First printing, 2018.

ISBN: 9781791725228

Library of Congress Control Number: 2018913807

About the author

Joyce Fennell, LMT. Aesthetician, Cosmetologist, Light worker, body worker, energy healer, empath and intuitive. Lifetime learner, teacher, and now author.

Acknowledgements

My heartfelt appreciation goes out to my editor, Abby White. She is a student editor who simply dropped into my life at the perfect time. I am grateful to her mother, Sydelle, for bringing us together. She is a long time client and friend.

Also I am in constant gratitude for my son James, who has spent countless hours working with me on this project.

I am ever grateful for all of the support I have received over these past years, from my family, friends and clients. Their support and belief in me means so much.

Thank you all. Peace.

Dedication

To my family

To my husband, Jim.

To my adult children, James and Jacqulyn.

And to the light of my life, my grandchildren, Brooke and Carter, who are my biggest fans.

Table of Contents

Prologue 1
Chapter 1: Listening to Ourselves 7
Chapter 2: Turning Purpose into Destiny 20
Chapter 3: Shifting Consciousness 37
Chapter 4: Working with Collective Energy 65
Chapter 5: Embracing the Universal Energy ... 81
Chapter 6: Living With Intention 103
Chapter 7: Connecting with the Higher Powers 114
Chapter 8: Trusting Your Inner Guidance 130
Epilogue 142

Prologue

You have a dream.

I know you do because everyone has a dream, whether they know it yet or not. Your soul entered your body for a reason: it is our responsibility, during our time on earth, to figure out what that reason is. Every person has a purpose — something they are here to do and be — and a destiny to fulfill.

I have learned that lesson through personal experience. When I was in high school, I wanted to become a broadcast journalist. Writing filled me up and allowed my creativity to expand. I wanted to use writing and reporting to meet people of different backgrounds, exploring all states of the human condition.

However, life happened. There was no talk of college in my household, and my grade point average was not high — until I signed up for cosmetology class.

Joyce Fennell

Through this course, I found a new way to fulfill my purpose of learning about and helping humanity. I earned a cosmetology license. After some years of practice, I had a calling to do something more. I studied Reiki, aromatherapy and energy healing modalities. I took metaphysical training and became a light-worker and intuitive. I received my massage therapy license and opened my own day spa. Today, I aid my clients in all aspects of health and wellness, mind, body, and spirit. The spiritual part of my practice is of the utmost importance to me. Aiding someone in their healing process fulfills my purpose. I am grateful every day to the higher power — God, Source, divine energy — who illuminated this path to fulfill my purpose and destiny, despite the obstacles I faced.

My soul has continued evolving and speaking to me. Its message is clear: my journey is not yet complete. I have learned and lived so much over the last years of my life that now; the lifetime learner must become the lifetime teacher. Would it be simpler to continue doing what I am doing? Of course. However, I must answer the call and step into a new light: a new way of working and sharing my gifts. I am stepping into my own light in order to help others step into their own light, as well. The brightest lights in our lives shine when we truly align with our destiny and purpose.

Awakening the Guru Within

To fulfill this purpose, I have returned to my early love: writing. My journey demonstrates that every step of our lives, every disappointment or milestone, happens for a reason. The path I took may seem indirect. However, my years of working in the spa industry, as well as the health and wellness field, have introduced me to so many different people and parts of the human condition. Those insights have made me a better writer, a better health and wellness practitioner, and a better person. Without my winding path, I would not have been prepared for this moment.

I have written this book to help as many people as possible pursue and manifest their own dreams. Throughout my career, I have worked with the energies of all-powerful, divine, and loving forces, which work in each of our lives. These energies are guiding lights that illuminate the paths before us; they warn us of danger and keep us on our journeys; they envelop us all.

These energies are subtle. To receive them, we must listen to our gut feelings and tap into the great wisdom inside ourselves. Only by Awakening our Gurus Within can we access these energies and follow the paths they have set for us.

I believe our Gurus Within — our inner voices of wisdom — come from the highest powers in our universe. In this book, I may refer to those powers as "the higher powers," "divine energy," "universal energy," or "source." While reading this material, please use your higher power or source in place of my words. These "higher powers," "divine energies," and "universal energies" can encompass God, life forces, Buddha, Krishna, Allah — whatever and whomever you look to for wisdom and strength. No matter what or who you call it, I believe this most powerful life-giving energy is the same.

Accessing this energy will help you realize all you need to know, be, and do. That information exists within all of us, waiting to be brought into the world. You may have a sense of your purpose and destiny already — and you may have been taught to ignore those feelings. Such thinking could not be more wrong. Your desire to do or be something more does not come from your ego: that desire is your soul speaking to you. You must honor your soul's voice, its message, and the lessons these energies bring you every day.

By listening to our Guru Within, we will not just change ourselves. We will change the world. Our planet is experiencing significant energy shifts right now, and all of them lead toward a higher good. When we choose to follow the positive energies, we create more peaceful, fulfilling, purposeful lives for ourselves and for everyone around us. We, the people, have the power to create lasting change on our planet. We must use that power, for humanity's sake.

The journey to your destiny may not always be easy. Sometimes, you may want to give up. No matter what, though, you must stay the course. Your future self and your loved ones will thank you. Begin living the life you are here live; begin doing what you, and only you, are here to do.

Through this book, I am following my own journey. I am embracing my destiny to be witnessed by all who read this and who encounter me in their lives. I am not here to question my destiny; I am just here to take the actions necessary to move forward.

I advise you to do the same. Let go of your fears, your doubts, and your insecurities. Listen to your soul's calling and begin moving forward.

Our time is now.

Joyce Fennell

Chapter 1: Listening to Ourselves

The Guru Within

Your soul existed long before your body did, in commune with the universal divine energies and higher powers. When your body was born, your soul chose to live within it, nestled in the core of your being. Here, your soul guards all the information you will ever need to know, ready and waiting to be accessed. Know that your soul does not just sit silently: it is speaking to you. If you listen, you will hear its voice, telling you what your purpose and destiny are and how to achieve them. When you listen to this inner voice, this deepest wisdom of your soul, you are communing with your *Guru Within*.

Joyce Fennell

Your Guru Within fills you with knowing, from your head (the logical mind) to the solar plexus (that gut feeling). We can feel this knowing through our entire bodies, but we may not always recognize it as knowing. You may feel butterflies in your stomach, a sense of sudden euphoria, heart racing, or tightness in your chest, throat, back, or jaw. These are all visceral feelings of knowing what is good or not, when to take action or when to pause. Your Guru Within sends you these physical signals to help you find your true purpose and destiny — the right and responsibility of each soul incarnated into a body. If we are listening to our feelings and thoughts, we can hear our Gurus' call, and follow the path set out for us.

However, listening to those forces can be challenging. Our thoughts and desires play in the endless chatter in our minds. This mind chatter runs in a tape loop. When you listen to all the messages in your tape loop, you will notice the same messages over and over again. Most of them are not positive, and the messages never stop. Amid this negativity, you may not be able to hear your Guru Within.

First, we must recognize which messages in our tape loop are not authentic to who we are and cut out them out. When that kind of message comes up, stop and say, "That is not who I am or what I believe," and replace that space with a more positive thought. Keep doing this. It will take some time to cancel these messages, as they have lived in your head, playing over and over again, for a long time. However, somewhere beneath all that chatter lies your Guru Within and its essential guidance. Your Guru's voice may sound like a whisper, and the other chatter in your mind may drown it out, but it is there. You just need to access it. As you begin creating positive thoughts to replace the negative ones in your tape loop, notice which of the positive thoughts feel truer to whom you are. These thoughts are messages from your Guru Within. You must keep listening to and sifting through this tape loop: the more you listen, the more you will hear.

To follow our Gurus Within, we must also learn to manage forces outside our bodies. People in your life — parents, teachers, or friends — may have taught you to ignore the feelings and thoughts from your Guru Within. They may not have understood these messages' importance. In all likelihood, they were taught to ignore these messages as well. I do not believe anyone set out to stop you from accessing this information with malice. Rather, people in your life did not know these messages' significance. A lot of us live our lives, maybe our entire lives, without listening to our inner voices.

Joyce Fennell

We chalk them up as a dream or fantasy — something other people do.

I am here to say that your inner voice is not just real: it holds the utmost importance. Your Guru Within is like your best friend — not the one who asks, "Are you really going to wear that dress?" but the one who says, "Go on, I've got your back." It pushes you to be a better you, supporting your hopes, wishes, and dreams, even when no one else will. These friends help us achieve our greatest potential, just as the Guru Within does. By listening to this voice, we can achieve our destinies: to do and be all we are here to do and be.

This fulfillment is your right as well as your duty. It's easier to go with the flow and do what everyone else is doing. However, if you choose to be average instead of pursuing your purpose and your knowing, other people may indeed suffer due to your action or inaction. Think of all the people who have shifted human consciousness: Jesus, Gandhi, Buddha, Mother Theresa, and Martin Luther King, Jr. None of them found their paths easy, but by fulfilling their destinies, they helped millions of people. Achieving your destiny does not just help you: it contributes to the greatest good of all humanity.

We must Awaken the sleeping giants within ourselves and begin accessing our Gurus Within. *You* are who you have been waiting for to change yourself and, ultimately, the world.

The Process of Awakening

However, we can only access our Gurus Within once we have Awakened. *Awakening* means being present enough in your life — listening, watching, learning — to receive your Guru's messages. This process of Awakening will unfold over time. Be patient with this process: the timing is exactly as it should be. You may learn in pieces, slowly or quickly; you may have a sudden epiphany — an 'aha' moment — or not. Take your Awakening as it comes. Stay in the present as much as you can. If you do not know what to do, pause and wait for more information and ask for clarity.

We cannot Awaken without acknowledging the changes in our lives we need to make. Sometimes, we get wrapped up in the chaos around us. Life can feel as though we are hamsters in a cage, running on a wheel, going nowhere. We seem to have too much to do and not enough time to do it — yet our to-do list is never complete, and rarely includes ourselves. At these times in our lives, we tend to lack focus. We do not and cannot think of another thing. I get it: I've been there.

Joyce Fennell

The problem with this is, we never slow down enough to enjoy what we are doing. Our minds keep thinking, thinking, thinking — and only about the many things on our list. Is this what our human experience should be about? We each have a purpose for being here, on this planet, at this time. I can state with certainty that we are not here to complete daily tasks. Yes, we all have to do them; however, these tasks must not guide all our actions and choices. We are born free, to follow our hopes, wishes and dreams. We must reclaim our freedom: to pursue our purpose and destiny, to do and be what we came here to do and be. Awakening allows us reclaim this freedom and manifest it in our lives.

People are opening channels within themselves like never before in our lifetimes. This opening allows us to connect with our Guru Within, that knowing part of ourselves, through our souls. Through our Guru Within, we can access the higher power's divine energy and all the information that comes with that access. That is the all-knowing part of each of us, which rumbles with excitement over ideas that have not fully formed yet. Awakening brings us to these thoughts and ideas if we surrender to the divine energies guiding us. We begin to feel so much excitement, joy, and hope. We begin to feel something greater than ourselves — a divine, god-like energy. A loving light, more pure and magnificent than anything we have ever felt before. It is a visceral feeling. When we feel that light in our bodies, the energies are calling us.

Awakening in this way is an inside job. It always has been and it always will be. You alone can access your personal guidance: no one else can do it for you. There may be people who can assist you on your journey, helping you understand the information you are receiving. Provided that these are people with great integrity and good intentions; they affirm that your thoughts, wishes, and dreams are guiding you to your best self. However, they cannot complete your journey for you. No one but you knows the path you should take. You cannot access the light and energies within yourself simply by taking a weekend seminar or studying with any spiritual teacher, guru, or healer. You alone must do your own work and follow your own path to Awakening your Guru Within.

Although we can learn from others' processes, no one journey is the same. What works for one person does not necessarily work for everyone. It is a good idea to try different practices to see what resonates with you. However, no one person, no matter how big their ego is, no matter how evolved they are or seem to be, is anything more than you are. We are, each and every one of us, made of flesh, blood, and energy. All of us must follow the same basic principles of eating, sleeping, and breathing. No one, no matter what anyone says or does, knows your path or your journey as you do.

Once you achieve Awakening, its benefits will surprise and even delight you. For the first time in your life, you may begin to feel your authentic self emerge. You will have a sense of purpose and peace; you may even feel you have come home at last. These feelings will make your inner changes apparent to others, allowing the people in your life see you in a brighter light. As you begin to answer your soul's call, your life will Awaken and expand in every area. And as you Awaken your Guru Within, others will begin to Awaken theirs as well, one Awakened soul after another.

How to Begin Awaken Ourselves

To Awaken, first, you must acknowledge the desire within yourself, burning deep and demanding change. It is there, of this I am sure. If you do not recognize it, ask for guidance. Begin by asking the questions, "Where does my soul want me to go? What is my purpose in this life? Can you show me the next step?"

Awakening the Guru Within

Begin opening those channels within yourself and your Guru Within will answer you. However, once you ask, you must allow yourself to hear the answers. You do have free will, after all, and you may block these messages without realizing it. Be mindful of your endless mind chatter so that you can hear the messages you need to hear. Begin looking at all the information you are receiving, on every level.

Start by paying close attention to your thoughts, feelings, and psychic hits — those sudden moments of knowing. These sensations can be subtle, like whispers. If you're not present and listening, you may miss the message entirely. However, it is vital to begin working with these messages: they are our guiding lights, which keep us working toward fulfilling our personal destinies. They may come through dreams, while meditating, driving, or taking a shower, on a walk, during a massage, while practicing yoga — anything you are doing in a relaxed or meditative state. You will feel the knowing in your gut and know it to be true, so clear and certain that you cannot deny it, although your logical mind may try.

When you receive these messages, first and foremost, you must listen to them and take action. Perhaps you'll pick up the phone to call a friend and find they've just called you: you've both listened to your Gurus Within. The first step can be that simple. By taking that first step of listening and responding, you honor your Awakening. Go further by processing these messages the moment you hear them. It takes only a few seconds to ask, "What's that about?", "Is this mine?" or "Where did that come from?" Then, file these questions and your answers away in your mind. If you'd like to record them, write them down in a journal. This practice may help you understand messages which you may not understand the first time you hear them. As you reflect on these messages later, you will begin to receive clarity on what they mean and how they relate to your journey.

Begin to notice the physical world as well. If you pay attention, you will see the world differently. Notice the beauty in nature, in things as ordinary as a budding flower or a tree. Find pennies from heaven: they may be everywhere, but you have to be looking for them to find them. Now that I am present with my surroundings, I find pennies all the time. Sometimes, you'll even experience *synchronicity*: you'll keep seeing or hearing the same message over and over again.

Thirteen years ago, right before and right after I finished my exams for my massage license, I saw dragonflies everywhere, for the first time in my life. I realized the higher powers were using this synchronicity to send me a message, so I flipped through my copy of *Animal Speak*, Ted Andrews' book about what animal's meanings are in your life, to find out the significance of dragonflies. I learned dragonflies symbolize the beginning or end of a two-year transformation cycle, and that made sense to me. The dragonflies symbolized the two years of study I had just completed to earn my massage license, and the transformation I was preparing to make: opening my own day spa, just five months after earning my license. Now, the dragonfly is the logo for my business, giving all my clients a message of light, healing, and transformation.

I still see dragonflies and pennies; my sister sees white feathers. What do you see? Your messages can come through anything. There are road signs, license plates, and billboards that speak to us if we are present enough to notice them; there are songs on the radio and books and magazines. Whatever speaks to you, listen to it. These messages come from a higher place: they are divine intervention, and we need to be awake enough to see and hear them. They convey the undeniable truth of who we are, who we have come here to be, and most importantly, what we have come to do.

That burning sense of "I must do this" is just a thought. By the time it becomes a desire, its energy is already in motion. The higher power has placed that desire in front of us; we need to learn to recognize and embrace it. This is Awakening in its simplest form: recognizing what the universe is asking us to do and taking the actions necessary bring it forward into our lives. Here, you have a choice. You can go willingly along the path the universe has laid out before you, or you can go kicking and screaming. No matter which choice you make, you are going.

Awakening will become easier the more mindful you are about receiving it. Acknowledge and take action on your thoughts and feelings to help yourself through the process. When I feel drained, for instance, my Guru Within is telling me I've stayed too long, wherever I am. Once I understand this, I know I need to pause: there is no shame, and every honor, in listening to this message and taking the action necessary. Sometimes, too, you may see your work thwarted by one obstacle after another. This is the universe's way of saying, "No, stop right there." Listen to this message from the universe: if it is meant to be, it will be. If not, something better will take its place. Only when we resist the universe's guidance, when we are not in alignment with our soul's purpose, do we suffer.

As you begin honoring the Awakening process, the messages in your mind and body will become more frequent and reliable. Trust that information and get out of the way. Notice just how much your inner voice is guiding you. Be mindful of that voice, keep your energy clear, listen to your Guru Within, and act when necessary. Take these steps before the universe forces you to take them. Your journey will benefit greatly, because you took positive action.

You need look no further than yourself for joy and purpose. They are not waiting in another class, a few pounds lost, or the perfect partner. That is the beauty of your Guru Within: there's a reason the spiritual leader Jean Houston suggested G.U.R.U. should stand for, "Gee, you are you!" The more you look outside yourself, the more your inner joy will elude you. It's an inside job: letting go of things we do not need so we may embrace the things we do, as we move forward in our journeys. Imagine yourself on monkey bars, letting go of one bar so you can grab the next one. This movement requires courage, strength, and confidence. More importantly, it requires trust — trust in yourself, trust in your life and trust in what life is giving you.

In spiritual circles, we often use a phrase: "Leap and the net will appear." When you leap toward your destiny, the universe will catch you. Believe and trust your guidance, your knowing, your Guru Within.

Chapter 2: Turning Purpose into Destiny

Answering Your Soul's Call

When snowflakes fall from the sky, they look the same — and, indeed, they are all made of frozen water. However, if you look closely at individual flakes, you will see each has a different pattern. Humans are similar. We all have skin, bones, and the same organs and systems, mostly in the same places. However, our inner minds, ideas, thoughts, experiences, our families and our journeys are all one-of-a-kind.

We have these differences because we are all here to do and be different things. Even identical twins have free will to choose their own paths based on the inner workings of their minds, bodies, spirits, and souls. Our

Awakening the Guru Within

souls found their own, unique purposes before they entered our bodies. We were chosen as an energetic match. Each of us chose our purposes before we came into this world; we may never fully remember making these choices. However, we all came here to live a purposeful life, achieving what we chose to do and be. All of this happened before we entered our physical bodies, when we were just energy.

You have the responsibility, for yourself and the world, to fulfill your unique purpose and destiny while you are here. If you do not, what ripple effects will you cause across the universe? We cannot know what will or will not happen because of our actions or inactions. Imagine a world without the influence of Martin Luther King, Jr., Gandhi, or Mother Theresa. These people risked their lives to fulfill their purposes and destinies, and in doing so, they brought awareness and aid to millions of people. What if they had stayed home?

You must choose to answer your soul's call to live your life's purpose. Your inaction will have consequences, whether you realize it or not. The consequence may be that you keep living in fear or the consequence may be that others suffer without your guidance. If you choose not to follow your purpose, you may always feel something is missing in your life.

This is an emptiness that nothing and no one can ever fill.

Only Awakening to your soul's desires can begin to fill that emptiness. Once you find your purpose, deep within yourself, you can access the information you need to fulfill your destiny.

This is your soul, crying out to be heard. Will you answer the call?

Finding Your Purpose

The first step in finding your purpose is recognizing the meaning in everything you do. Whether you complete a mundane task or a grand gesture, check in with yourself and the action you took. Find what your intention in that action was. You must find the meanings in all your actions. This journey of self-discovery will bring you to the deepest parts of yourself: your all-knowing soul, the Guru Within.

This is how you begin to access your personal destiny and live the life you are here to live. No one on the planet is here to do what you are here to do. Some may have similar journeys, and some may launch projects such as books, companies, and songs that you wish you could have launched. The truth is, though, you *could* have launched them. The divine energies put creations into the universal energy, waiting to be realized. Whoever recognizes those energies and takes the required actions first, are the ones who bring the project to life. A universal intelligence brings these messages forward, but you must choose to be the vehicle from which they launch.

There are also certain things that are yours alone to do. If you do not make them happen, no one will. You must answer the universe's call to action, even when you stand on the edge of the unknown. When you do — when an action is right for both you and the universe — you will know it in every fiber of your being. The action you choose will begin to take on a life of its own.

Think of overnight sensations: totally, completely unknown people catapulted into success, like the contestants on shows such as *American Idol*. After lifetimes of anonymity, these people suddenly become famous for their talent. Their success is no mistake. For a few of them, success may have been as easy to achieve as it looks to the outsider. However, most of those new stars have likely pursued their destinies in some way or another for a very long time. Until now, that journey may have happened within them, but once they have achieved fame, their journeys have externalized. It's like when you get a new haircut.

People notice your outward change, but in all likelihood, that haircut is part of an inner journey that has been going on for some time now. The haircut just shows that journey outwardly.

But whether you're competing on a televised talent show or changing your hairstyle, you have to take that first step. Some people may feel they can stay home, meditate, and pray, and something will just drop into their laps. I have seen people try these tactics, and I can say they are still at home, waiting. Yes, meditation and prayer can be excellent tools; however, a dream without action is just a dream, never realized. Too many people rely on the Law of Attraction: the principle that we can attract energies and effects just by thinking about them, by creating a vision in our minds' eye that we want to bring forth. This principle is powerful, but your destiny cannot and will not happen unless you are an active, conscious participant in it. That is the spiritual law.

Start with simple steps. Don't let your life be a carnival ride, running from one rush to another, always on the chase for the next high. No one benefits from the chaos you'll create, least of all you. Instead, stop and ask yourself, "What am I creating in my life right now? Is this in line with what I want?" Sit with those questions; be silent and reflective. Ask your Guru

Awakening the Guru Within

Within and the higher powers for wisdom and pause. Their answers may appear as a whisper, becoming louder and clearer as the process unfolds before you. Do not try to rush this process. Be mindful of all of the information you are receiving and how it makes you feel, deep within the core of your being.

During this reflection, you may realize you have had thoughts, wishes, and dreams about things related to your destiny and purpose. You may feel a burning desire, a longing and a knowing, which gives you a sense of clarity you have never known before. This is the right message: you can feel it. Honor these moments of clarity and take action on them. The logical mind may want to get in your way, and it probably will. In that case, you will need to move forward even if it creates discomfort, uncertainty, or fear within your own being. When you look into the face of fear, fear has no power over you. You must take your power back from fear; you must not let anyone or anything take your power from you again.

Once you know the purpose you need to fulfill, you must consider your next steps. You may need to take additional training or find more information, especially if your purpose is a new interest or experience for you. Some of the next steps you might take — actions like reading books, meditating, signing up for a seminar, or sending an email — involve little to no risk. Other times, you might need to risk more to get more. More often than not, however, we do not need to learn anything else: we already have everything we need, because we have been drawn to certain things throughout our lives. *Aha!* There is our purpose, of course — it's been there the whole time. We have taken the classes and learned the lessons, and when the moment comes, we are ready. Your Guru Within will reveal the steps and risks you need to take. Listen to your Guru and trust it. Our Awakenings happen in divine order. Life is always working to show us our purpose and destiny, even if we have spent years denying or avoiding these messages.

Your journey may not always be direct. Mine has not been, and often, when I have gotten off-track, my life has felt more difficult. However, we all slip off-track at times, and we can learn great lessons in those moments. Do not let the things that happen to you define you; let your choices define you instead. Accept what is happening, whether it is difficult or easy, and ask, "What am I to learn from this?" Listen for the answer. Pick yourself up, brush yourself off, and get right back on track. Do not let your fears and insecurities paralyze you into inaction. Do not let anyone get in the way of your destiny.

Awakening the Guru Within

You are the one you have been waiting for: no one knows your purpose or destiny like you do. Some may question what you are thinking or doing; let their negativity bounce off of you. It cannot stick to you if you do not own it as yours. The time to act is now: once your authentic self has Awakened within you, you may not get another chance. If you do nothing, nothing happens; if you do something, something will happen. That is the spiritual law.

I am asking you to co-create your life with the divine energies. You must make that choice consciously. Following your life's purpose may mean walking down the road less traveled, and that walk may be more difficult than you think. However, when you pursue your destiny, your life will unfold for you in the exact way you laid it out before you came here. Be patient: let this path emerge one step at a time. Pay close attention to what is happening in all areas of your life. This process may take a lifetime; however, you must stay the course. It is a worthwhile journey and a necessary one. The rewards will be great. By illuminating your true self, you may feel as though you have just met yourself for the first time. You may feel as if you have finally come home, recognizing a part of yourself so deep within you that you did not even know it existed, until now.

Joyce Fennell

Persevering with Purpose

Once you find your purpose, you begin the process of manifesting your destiny. This process is of the utmost importance. Imagine meeting the higher powers' divine energy at the Gates of Heaven and being asked, "Why did you not live out your destiny and purpose?"

You cannot answer that you didn't have the time, money, or whatever excuse you can come up with. No fears or doubts can outweigh the benefits to ourselves and to the universe of fulfilling our destinies. Instead, you must overcome the challenges which keep you from living out your destiny and purpose.

Many of those challenges involve other people. Do not sabotage yourself by giving your power away. Sometimes, our friends and family can help us; other times, however, they can feel like negative forces, trying to get in our way. They may not even realize what they are doing, and they may think they are protecting you. Please, do not let your past experiences with people make you dismiss what they say outright. Listen to them, consider what they are saying, and make a decision based on contemplation. You must do the same for people in your life who want to hold you back for their own reasons. They will teach you as well.

Awakening the Guru Within

These relationships show you the yin and yang of life: pushing and pulling, light and darkness. Finding your balance and boundaries with these people may be one of the biggest challenges in your life, and may well teach you the biggest lessons. Be strong enough in your beliefs and spiritual practice not to let anyone take away your power or get in the way of your life's purpose.

During your Awakening, there may be things you do not tell those people closest to you. Sometimes it's easier to be on a solo journey, working with intention and purpose, instead of dealing with the anxieties of those who have not yet Awakened. However, you must also remain open to the people who will be able to help you on your journey. You will meet people who will guide you, showing you new ways of looking at the world and exposing you to the people and things you need to know. These new friends and mentors have something to teach you, and you have something to teach them in return. Their entry in your life is not a chance encounter or a coincidence: the divine energies have brought them to you. It is fate. The higher powers show you what you need to know, when you need to know it. Trust them. Everything that happens in your life is part of the plan your soul chose with the divine energies before you were born. Never lose sight of that.

Joyce Fennell

You must also never lose sight of your purpose, no matter what physical obstacles arise. Sometimes family, health, or work issues come up, and we do need to attend to our physical lives. It is part of our earth walk to be set off-course sometimes. When these setbacks occur, we may need to step back and pause. However, we must not lose sight of our ultimate purpose and destiny. Consider what we can learn from these setbacks. Maybe they are necessary, so that we can pause and integrate what we have learned so far into our forward movement. When the crisis has passed, we will pick up where we left off and continue on our journeys. We may even be more ready than ever.

No matter what, be true to yourself and to the journey of discovering your full self. This journey is yours most of all. Acknowledge your thoughts, wishes, and dreams. Do not squash them, disregard them, or think them impossible. As we become more and more Awakened to these deep desires, the path to fulfillment will appear before us. Embrace the idea that such fulfillment is already yours and realize that you need to take action. Without action, a dream is just a dream, unrealized. When you take action, that dream takes flight and becomes a reality. Of this, I am certain.

Manifesting Your Destiny

Manifesting your destiny may seem or feel impossible, but it's not. I have laid out this process in seven steps. How to manifest your destiny:

1. Ask for what you need, aloud or silently.
You can ask for something specific, like a new job, or for something more general, like new, positive energies. In either case, you must *ask*. Unless you ask for something, you cannot receive it. Ask for what you desire to create aloud or in prayer, in conversations or alone: if it is yours to have, because it serves your destiny and purpose, you will receive it. Be brave in your asking. Know that you may need to keep asking. You may receive what you need the first time you ask, or you may not. Only the divine energy knows. If the thing you are asking for is not in line with your destiny and purpose, you may find yourself pushing too hard for it, whatever it is. You will not receive it. If that happens, learn from your futility: stop pushing to create something that is not yours to have. Step away and allow what is yours to come in. Be open to what the higher powers give you, even if it's not what you expected. Quite possibly, your destiny and purpose exceed your expectations.

2. Visualize what you desire to create in as much detail as possible. See and feel yourself receiving it.

Make a movie reel in your mind's eye. See the things you are asking for; see yourself receiving them. Then imagine, physically, exactly what that manifestation feels like. How does receiving that gift feel in your body, in your gut? What feelings does it evoke within you? A sense of peace, a coming home. A sense of joy and contentment, even euphoria. Allow your body to see and feel receiving these gifts from the divine energies. Allow yourself to feel and know these gifts are what you are here to receive. Know these gifts have everything to do with where you are going in your life and how you will get there.

You can use the physical world to help yourself imagine receiving the things you have asked for. Let's say you want a specific car. Go to the dealership and drive the car you would like to have. Feel the seats; feel the ride. Is it smooth? Is it bumpy? Smell that new car smell. As you drive this car, feel it as yours, in your physical body, and own it in your energy. Feel the vibration it stirs within you and keep that vibration as you go about your life. Thoughts and things have their own vibrations: you must be mindful of your vibrations and of the vibrations you wish to attract. By matching your vibration with the vibration of the thing you want, you will bring that thing into your life.

3. *Talk about your purpose. Put your energy out into the universe.*

By giving voice to hopes, wishes, and dreams, you supercharge them: you put the vibration of what you are asking for into the universal energies. Your asking begins vibrating and attracting similar energies. For this reason, you must not keep your purpose a secret; you must talk about it to someone. No matter what your purpose is, or how crazy it might sound to your family, friends, and even yourself, you must speak about it. Now, let me caution you here: do not tell your ideas to people who only give you negative feedback. If need be, talk to people who have no vested interest in the outcome of what you are creating in your life. Talk to yourself or to your guides; talk to the higher powers' divine energy, your counselor, or your dog. Talk to whoever will listen. At the early stages, you don't need to speak in great detail. You are putting the energy out there, not keeping it bottled up inside: that's what matters. These ideas need room to expand and grow into the awesome destiny you seek.

4. *Act as if you already have what you are asking for —
   because, energetically, you already do.*

At the end of the day, your destiny is just energy. You simply need to access it. Sometimes, you may need a sign from the universe — a literal sign, like a street sign, or a figurative one, like my dragonflies — to realize what your destiny is. This realization will start in your creative mind as an idea, a thought, a psychic hit, or an 'aha' moment. Once you begin Awakening to your destiny, bring this knowing from your mind's eye into your solar plexus — that gut feeling deep in your core. Feel what it will feel like to have your destiny manifest. Then, bring that feeling from the core of your being — your gut, your soul self, your Guru Within — all the way back up into your mind's eye. Let that feeling spread into every part of your being. Allow that feeling to radiate from your physical body into the energy of all things. As you go out into the world, be mindful of your energy. Radiate this fulfilled, successful energy as if you already have it. Own it as yours, and it will drop into your life – Almost magically.

5. *Be in gratitude for receiving all you are receiving.*

Say "Thank you" for your destiny, your energies, and the things you are creating in your life. Be in gratitude and feel yourself receiving them, right here, right now. When you achieve gratitude at this level, two energies — the energy of what you are asking for and the energy of gratitude for receiving it — meet before your very eyes. When these energies meet and begin vibrating at the same level, you receive what is yours to have. Say "Thank you" again and again, not just for receiving what you have received, but for receiving everything that follows as well. This gratitude is essential for receiving your destiny and purpose.

6. *Be present with the process.*

It is of the utmost importance to be present with the process of manifesting your destiny. Sometimes, the process may feel and seem easy; other times, it may be more challenging. This presence takes patience and practice. Soon enough, you will be present in all things. Be present with yourself, for yourself, the way you would be for your best friend, going through a transformative time in life. That is your Guru Within: your own best friend, inside you. As you manifest your destiny, support yourself without being judge and jury of every step. Make your missteps teachable moments whenever you can. Know you can achieve as much growth in the difficult times as in the good ones. Often, even when you feel like nothing is happening, in that blank space between creation and manifestation, so much is happening.

7. *Be a force for good.*

What greater gift is there than being fully present with yourself and the people around you? When you choose to be present with your process, you are choosing to pursue your highest, best self. The closer you get to that goal, the more good you will bring to the world. Our presence with ourselves is a gift to every other person we encounter. Choose in each and every moment to be a force for good: a higher, brighter, better consciousness. It is truly your choice.

As you become more Awakened and present in your life, those around you will begin to Awaken as well. When the people around them start to Awaken, this Awakening will ripple around the world. That is what we are here to do: become Awakened, realized beings, and help others do the same. The power of us Awakening will shift the energy of our world. As individuals, we can use this inner power to create great change. We do have the power.

Chapter 3: Shifting Consciousness

Living Consciously

What has become clear to me, and perhaps to you as well, is the unconscious way we live on this planet. Despite our knowledge, education, technology, and the energy that sustains us, we live day to day in a non-present state. Particularly in American culture, we eat, spend, drink, and pollute every day, often without giving thought to our actions. We see the consequences of that unconsciousness around us every day. All over the news and in our personal lives, we see people feeling unsettled and looking again at things that happened in the past, perhaps to make sense of everything happening in the present. We feel surrounded by chaos and disorder, blocked physically, emotionally, spiritually, and energetically.

We have the power to change that reality. We must begin living conscious lives. Individually and collectively, we can shift the consciousness of ourselves, one another, this country, and ultimately the world, one person at a time. The time is now: no more sitting on your thoughts, wishes, and dreams; no more playing the victim or complaining about the way life is. The time is now to get out of your chair, take some action, and make a difference. Know the universal energy continues to move us in the direction of a better, more Awakened life and self.

Those of us who are Awake and Awakening feel the huge energetic shift happening on our planet. The higher powers' divine energies are calling upon us to assist others through this time of energetic chaos. I feel that shift happening right now. If you do not yet, soon, you will, too.

However, you must listen to the higher powers carefully. Sometimes, their call may not come directly to us. We may hear the higher powers through others instead. Children, especially, bring us innocence, joy, and love straight from the higher powers' divine energies. Our roles in our children's lives are crucial, as are their roles in ours. We must help them rise to meet their destinies. It is our duty and our privilege. They are the higher powers' divine energy of love and light, and they are here to illuminate our lives and our planet.

Either we are contributing to the greater good by helping our children, ourselves and our communities, or we are taking up space and valuable resources. Who will you choose to be? Someone who is living and working toward the highest good of our world, or someone using up vital resources for the glory of your own, egoic self?

We must choose the former path, toward the highest good. The Awakening of ourselves and, more importantly, our planet, has been happening for years. I am excited about the possibilities in store for all of us, and I believe the greater good will rise, victorious, from this time of Awakening. Yes, we will meet great challenges and obstacles as our collective consciousness shifts. However, when we work together, co-creating a better world, we will find a way forward. A new reality will emerge: a better place to live, love, and raise our families.

Isn't that what we all want? A better future for ourselves, our children, and their children?

We must realize that the better future is not always easy. Sometimes, human thoughts, emotions, and circumstances cause us to stray from the more

Awakened parts of ourselves. Personal pain can set us off-course, even when we have not physically suffered. The deaths of loved ones, for example — those who lived full lives, or those who seemed too young or healthy to have their lives cut short — devastate us. Take comfort in knowing that only your loved ones' bodies have left the world. The higher powers' divine energy may have known your loved ones needed to ride the new energies as free spirits. They may have needed your loved ones' spirits elsewhere to aid the shifts happening right now.

Whatever the answer, you must look to the new, conscious world coming toward us. Do not dwell on the time you strayed from your path, and do not blame yourself for straying. Pain is part of the human experience. It is unavoidable. Once your painful period has passed and you feel ready, get up, brush yourself off, and begin moving forward again. Remember the lessons you learned during your detour, staying mindful of where you are and where you are going. Keeping your thoughts on the best possible outcome, and step by step, you will achieve it.

That journey requires us to step up. Whatever burning desire you have within yourself — not the self-serving, egoic self, but your true self — it is time to take action. For a long time, you may have ignored the voice of your Guru Within, asking to be noticed, heard, and honored. Start listening. You have no more time to waste. Embrace what is, and allow the old to fall away. Holding on too tightly to things from the past will only harm you. Let go and let the divine energies guide you instead: it's like riding with the stream of life, coasting on its waves. Swimming against the current will only harm you, and ultimately, the current will win. You can choose to jump into the stream and allow the water to lead you willingly, or you can choose to swim against the current, resisting change. Either way, you are going.

Choose the path of least resistance. We must not lose energy keeping something alive that holds us back and needs to be released. Release the things you do not need in order to free yourself to pursue your brightest future.

Stepping Out of Unconscious Life

To start living consciously, first, we must understand what conscious living is. It's the opposite of *unconscious* living: being on auto pilot in your life. You act and react without much thought for what happens next. It's like living with blinders on, giving no thought to the consequences of your actions beyond that moment.

Joyce Fennell

Think about how we as a culture spend money. You probably use a credit card. With one swipe, you can spend any amount of money without pausing to consider the consequences of your purchase. It's just that easy: with one, magic card, you can have *it*, whatever *it* is in that moment. However, the things you buy will never bring you lasting joy. You may feel happy at first, but once that rush wears off, you'll just need to buy more. When you swipe and swipe, you're spending unconsciously, without considering whether your purchase is worth your money in the long run.

In conscious living, you spend money — you engage in all actions — with more intention. Instead of using credit cards, you may want to pay for your expenses in cash. Count out the dollars. Put each expense in an envelope. Dealing with money by hand, seeing it in front of you, will impact your life in a powerful way. That intentionality puts your spending into a whole new perspective, helping you make only meaningful purchases in the future. Conscious living can even change the way you think: when you are fully present in a moment, you can cut thoughts which do not serve a higher purpose out of your mind chatter as soon as you notice them.

You may ask yourself where you act unconsciously in your own life. Maybe you eat and drink without considering how you'll feel tomorrow; maybe you attend events out of habit even though you have outgrown your interest in them. Be mindful and check in by asking yourself: "Will this drink give me a hangover, making me late for work? Will this event take time away from doing something I would enjoy doing — something that would support my energy?" Unless you ask these questions, you will never discover the answers to them that lie within you. This process will lead you to the larger questions that need your mindful attention.

Sometimes, I also mentally observe myself to learn how I act unconsciously. In a given moment, visualize yourself stepping out of your body and watching your circumstances play out. Embrace a feeling of detachment, as if you are watching a movie, and watch yourself without judgment. Through this self-observation, you can acknowledge which of your behaviors are intentional and which are not. Such consciousness illuminates your path to transformation: choose to live consciously today, tomorrow, and in every moment of every day.

The time for significant change is *now* in our lives, in the lives of those we touch, and in our world. We must lay down any judgments, criticisms, doubts, and fears we have. This is the time to forgive ourselves for being more than spirits — for being human.

How to move into conscious life:

1. *Forgive yourself.*

Wow, that's big. Let's do this step together. First, collect any and all of your negative self-talk, guilt, regrets, shame, blame, indiscretions, imperfections, and harsh self-judgments. Put these thoughts and feelings in a container in your mind. Visualize your container — a vase, a wooden box, or a crystal bowl, perhaps — and imagine it in your mind's eye. If you want, you can also make a literal container, filled with the negative thoughts and feelings you have written on paper. Then, destroy the container. Throw it out, bury it, or burn it. Banish these negative thoughts and feelings from your mind and forgive yourself for all of them, past, present, and future.

2. *Forgive others.*

Start forgiving others by learning the art of *allowing*. Allow others to start Awakening and living consciously. Forgive them for ways they harmed you in the past or present: do not allow yourself feel negativity from that source anymore. Holding onto old pains and resentments only harms you. Forgiving people who have wronged you in the past does not make what they said or did okay. However, through your acts of forgiveness, you forgive and free yourself. You must enact this forgiveness physically, emotionally, spiritually, and on your soul level. Ultimately, bringing this peaceful energy back to yourself will increase your personal energy and vibration.

3. *Remove the energies holding you back.*

Once you have forgiven yourself and others, you must accept what you cannot change: others' actions, past or present. However, you can change yourself, and the people around you will change toward you or move away from you. Allow these changes to happen. Do not hold onto people who would hold you back from your purpose. You must remove their negative energies — a challenging task, but a necessary one. Perhaps in the future, some of these people will reenter your life; others will not. We must trust the higher powers' divine energy to bring the people we need back to us.

As you remove those negative energies and step into conscious living, remember to be in gratitude for any information you are receiving from the universe. Do not say, "Well, I didn't expect my future to look like that. No, thanks." You must reflect on what the universe is giving you. It may be just a glimpse of possibilities, or it may be a call to action. If you are asking to receive, you must receive what comes, the way it comes. Do not make quick decisions based on old patterns and fears. Instead, make decisions based on staying true to your own purpose and destiny. Your answers will come with each step of your path as it unfolds in front of you. Listen closely to those answers.

All the while, remember: you have free will. You can choose to listen and take the actions necessary or not; you can choose to stray off your path or stay on it. Remember the power of your choices as you fulfill your purpose and destiny. If you do nothing, nothing happens; if you do something, something happens. Life is a journey, not a destination, and the choices you make will reflect themselves in the life you are living now. Choose to sit in the driver's seat of your life. If you want to make a significant change, shift the way you think and make conscious choices moving forward.

Surrendering to Your Destiny

What does *surrendering* mean? To use a cliché: "Let go, let God." A lot of truth lies in this statement. Sometimes, you must surrender to *what is* instead of *what could be*. This is not about giving up your dream: surrendering does not mean quitting. Rather, when you surrender, you stop spending energy trying to change something you must accept. You will begin to move forward when you surrender to where you are now: you must go through it to get through it. Surrendering activates our own power, moving us forward and opening us up to something greater than ourselves.

As in any twelve-step program, you must start by accepting your problem: "I am an addict," for example, or "I do not the direction my life is going." You cannot create real change until you acknowledge where your life is right now — or, in the words of an ancient Navajo proverb, "You can't wake a person that is pretending to be asleep." Be honest with yourself as you tackle whatever is holding you back. *Surrender* and *acceptance* are the first steps to moving from where you are to where you are going.

You must continue surrendering as you pursue your purpose. Are you trying to force something to happen? Allow life to work for you and unfold in front of you instead. Be present where you are; otherwise, you will miss what is happening now in the quest to find what might be. If you stay present and conscious, you will receive lessons in every moment of your life. Surrender to a lesson the moment you receive it, and allow the lesson play out without deciding if it is a good thing or a bad one. It just *is*. Given enough time, this moment will pass, and another lesson will follow.

Sometimes we just have to state aloud: "I surrender to what is, right here, right now." Make no judgment about the moment you are experiencing. Later, you may reflect on the moment and see more clearly what lessons you have learned then. Look at your hand, right in front of your face: it's blurry, with its details obscured. As you move your hand farther away, you begin to see it more clearly. The same is true for life and the lessons we are here to learn. As you step away from a situation, it is then you will see it more clearly.

I believe that when we limit our dreams to what we know consciously, we may not realize all the possibilities life is giving us. That's why we must surrender to all that will be: you may be surprised and delighted by how far you will go. Do not put conditions on this process. Do not say, for example, that you will surrender if you find a partner or get a new job. Just surrender fully, on faith alone, and see your authentic self and your path to a purposeful life emerge. Quite possibly, you will go beyond anything you could have ever imagined or dreamed for yourself.

Awakening the Guru Within

Banishing What Harms You

We can develop harmful thoughts and feelings from any number of sources. Even our loved ones — parents, teachers, friends, siblings — can say things that stick in our energies, without realizing their impacts on our lives. Engaging your mind consciously gives you the chance to remove these negative energies. Harmful thoughts and feelings can grow into something like a cancer in the mind, body, and spirit. You have to defeat that cancer; otherwise, it affects all you see, do, and experience. Without those harmful thoughts and feelings, you can embrace new, positive energies. You can open yourself to a more fulfilling life. However, to do this, you must first *banish* the old, harmful thoughts and feelings once and for all. Are you ready?

To begin with, collect any and all harmful, judgmental, depressing, or negative thoughts you may have. By any and all, I mean it: thoughts, memories, emotions, beliefs, dreams, disappointments, and more. When you identify a thought which may be harmful, ask yourself, "Am I losing energy to this? Is this taking my joy away?" You can feel the answer to this question. Harmful thoughts drain your energy, like leaving your car's lights on all night. They can also cause feelings such as stress, anger and despair, or physical symptoms, such as headaches and upset stomachs. If a thought drains your energy or presents you one of these symptoms and your answer is "Yes", then that thought is harmful to you.

Acknowledge that you have these harmful thoughts and set an intention to release them from your physical, emotional, and spiritual body. By setting your intention, you create a powerful energy around the negative charge that lives within you. Then, you must act on your intention. Create a box in your mind and put all your harmful thoughts and feelings inside it. You may want to create a literal box as well. For this exercise, write your thoughts and feelings on pieces of paper. As you sort these harmful thoughts and feelings, say aloud:

"Into this box, I place all the old thoughts, ideas, beliefs, and any and all things in my life that no longer serve me. I release them to the higher powers' divine energy with love, kindness, and gratitude for all the lessons they have brought me. I release them without judgment to the universal energy, to be cleansed and banished from my life. I now reclaim this energy for myself. I look forward with hope and embrace the fullness of who I am."

As you set your intention to release and be released from these energies, you may want to burn, bury, or

Awakening the Guru Within

tear up the papers in your box. Do this as a physical manifestation of what you are asking the universe to do for you internally. Then, bring in the universal energy through the top of your head. With this goodness and light, draw the energy fully into your physical body, into each and every cell.

Now, imagine a golden-white ball of light in your third-eye chakra, in the center of your forehead. Imagine the ball has a sticky surface. Allow the ball to move through your physical body, from the top of your head to the bottom of your feet. This sticky ball is picking up anything that no longer serves you: thoughts, emotions, beliefs, even physical ailments. You may not be ready to release some of these areas, and that's okay. Do not let the ball get stuck there. Keep the ball moving, picking up any and all toxic sludge within your physical and spiritual body. When you have finished, bring the golden-white ball into the soles of your feet and release this energy into Mother Earth. Say out loud, with gratitude and grace, "I release this energy and its charge into the Great Mother to hold, for it no longer serves me in this life. Amen." You may also do this exercise in the shower: imagine your old energies flowing down the drain.

Once you have finished that process, imagine a golden-white light of healing energy. Bring that energy from the Heavens into the top of your head and allow it to move through your whole body. Bathe each and every cell, muscle, tissue, and organ in your body with this golden-white light of healing, the love of the divine. Feel your new reality: the lightness in your physical, emotional, and spiritual body. Sit with this new energy, embrace your new reality, and be in gratitude, always.

Spreading Your New Energy

It is up to you to bring this new energy into your part of the world and affect all those with whom you come into contact. We can and will make a difference by choosing the energy we carry with us. Spreading positive energy is how we can create change — not just for ourselves, but also for our community, our country, and the universe.

With your new energy, you will notice that new opportunities and people will begin to enter your life. Your energy will guide you to the people, places, and things that will catapult you into the next phase of your life. You will begin a whole new path, one that makes you feel like you are part of something much bigger than yourself. Embrace all these new possibilities with

Awakening the Guru Within

wonder and joyfulness. They are bringing you closer to your authentic self.

Once you start living in the present moment, it will take practice to stay present. However, some simple techniques can help us live consciously in every moment.

How to practice presence:

Practice 1: Scan

Write "I am practicing presence" on pieces of paper. Post these signs in places where you will see them all the time, such as your car, kitchen, bathroom, or desk. Every time you see these signs, read them and center yourself in the present moment. Do a body scan: how are you feeling? How does your body feel? Are you energized or tired? Does anything hurt? Do you feel healthy and strong? What does your mind have to say right now? Are you here now, or are you thinking about yesterday or tomorrow? Just notice, without judgment. Remember you cannot change what you do not recognize or acknowledge.

Now, bring yourself back into the moment. Be where you are. How do your clothes feel against your body? What are you standing or sitting on? Observe your surroundings. What do you love about this place? How does the energy feel? Quiet your mind; do not let mind chatter enter. See, touch, hear, taste, and smell. Breathe consciously. Give yourself the gift of you, in the way you give yourself to others. Receive your own essence. Begin feeling at home, at last.

Practice 2: Photograph

You can also practice presence by taking a photo in your mind. In any situation, look around closely; you may even blink your eyes like a camera lens. Imprint that moment into your mind and experience it fully. Let it develop into an image. Afterwards, you can always look back at that photo in your mind, where you have captured it forever. The first time I did this for myself was at my daughter's bridal shower, where all her guests painted tiles to make into a heart-shaped mirror for her. I took an imaginary photo of all my daughter's closest friends and family painting, talking, and laughing together. Now, I have that photo stored in my memory forever. It's not lost in the millions of moments in my mind; it's here for me to access anytime.

I often advise brides to take these photos as the doors open for their wedding ceremony. Before you walk down the aisle, stop and look around. See and feel the love in the room. Take that moment as your own, and take a mental photo of what you see and feel. From my experience with brides, it may be the only moment you remember from the day. Imagine if you were truly present for your entire wedding day. How amazing would that be?

Practice 3: Ask

Here's another idea to practice presence. Ask yourself throughout the day: "Am I present?" Check in with yourself. When your mind is somewhere else, notice where you are and why you are there. Draw yourself back into the present. Imagine a beautiful silk scarf around your waist and gently pull the scarf back toward yourself. We all let our thoughts drift away from the present moment sometimes — maybe even most of the time. There is no shame in having to remind ourselves to stay in the here and now. Practicing presence means being mindful of where we are and what we are thinking about. It means recognizing and coming back to the place we are now, in the present moment.

Malcolm Gladwell, in his book *Outliers*, discussed the 10,000 Hour Rule. The 10,000 Hour Rule posits that you need to practice something for ten thousand hours to master it. That number may seem daunting: one year has just 8,760 hours! In other words, if you practice 24/7, it will just take over a year to be fully present. But the practice itself matters more than the hours we spend practicing. If we practice with focus and commitment, we will not need a year to master staying in the present. Sometimes, achieving such mastery will seem impossible; however, those moments are the ones which force you to stretch beyond conflict into growth.

Use the exercises in this book as much as you need to. You are rising above the way humans have lived — unconscious lives, filled with chaos — for thousands of years. We cannot change this practice entirely in a day, a week, or even a year. However, we can begin to shift our own consciousness right now, one moment at a time. Never forget that you are a work in progress. If you stumble or fall, pick yourself up, brush yourself off, and move forward. Remain confident and committed to being present for all things in your life.

Living without Fear

As you move forward, you will confront fear. We all do. In times of danger, fear can save our lives; however, most of the time we are not in danger. In these times, fear can paralyze us. Our world makes it easy to feel this most useful and debilitating emotion. The news never runs out of dramatic events: wars, the economy tanking, incoming storms, even criminals in our

Awakening the Guru Within

neighborhoods. Religious groups can create a fear-based culture, too, claiming you will receive divine punishments if you disobey their laws.

However, some fears hit closer to home, and begin to take root at the beginning of our lives. As we grow up, a lot of negative things *do* happen. We need to acknowledge and accept those things in order to heal ourselves. Yet we also feel less tangible fears. We have become afraid of not being good enough, not making enough money, being alone — the list goes on.

Are these rational fears? No: they are just thoughts that run through your subconscious over and over, like a broken record. We don't even realize these thoughts are recurring, yet they hurt us deeply over time. The good news is that we have the power to leave our lives of fear. When you live consciously, you will begin to understand which fears are real and which are not. You will learn how to move through your fears in order to achieve your brightest future.

Let's think through a fearful situation together. For instance, ask yourself: "What will happen if my partner leaves me?" We know what will happen first: you will feel immense pain. You may need to seek professional help to get through it, and there is no shame in that. You may also have to change your lifestyle; you may have to move, or share custody of your children. For a while, life will challenge you, and you will continue feeling grief and loss. However, one day, you will find yourself on the other side of your pain and realize you are okay. You may even realize that you are better and stronger than before.

We have wasted too much energy living in fear. Most fear is irrational, and most of what we fear never happens to us. When we run from fear, it chases us. However, when we face fear head on, we disempower it. Begin moving forward with the absence of fear. As your fear fades, parts of you will grow into something new — something better. The choice is yours: continue to live in fear or go fearlessly forward, powerful and free.

The time is now to choose to be extraordinary in all areas of your life. Affirm your new path. Say out loud, "I choose to go fearlessly into the next phase of my life!"

The Power of Living Consciously

That next phase of life is conscious living. Choose to live consciously in everything you do — thoughts, actions, and reactions alike. To begin, use a powerful "I am" statement, such as, "I am choosing to live consciously every day in every way." Reaffirm this

Awakening the Guru Within

commitment to yourself as often as you need to. This is a lifelong process that you will develop and refine over your lifetime.

When making "I am" statements, I am reminded of something I once heard: "Whatever follows 'I am' is coming for you." I think the entire planet needs to hear that. What this means is that when you say or think something, you are bringing that energy into your life. Ask yourself what "I am" statements you are telling yourself. Are you telling yourself that you are unhealthy, lonely and broke? Or are you telling yourself that you are healthy, happy, abundant, and in good relationships? Reflect on those statements and begin to change the message if you need to. Choose conscious living and keep choosing it. This can feel like a seismic shift in your life. We must continue choosing consciousness until it becomes our new normal.

First, let your senses guide you. Pay close attention to what you see, hear, feel, and even taste. You are one body moving on a planet with billions of people. Every one of those people has a physical, emotional, and spiritual body within and around them. Those bodies send out energies, and those energies bump into all of us in some way. When someone feels depressed, that energy goes out into the world; when someone feels joyful or loving, those energies go out into the world as well. We bump into these energies all day long without realizing it. Have you ever walked into a room, for example, and suddenly known something was wrong? You could just feel it energetically. You have bumped into someone or something's energies, and sure enough, they have affected your mood. For your sake and others', pay attention to both the energies around you and the energies you are vibrating into the world. Embrace the good energies you find and walk away from negative ones.

Years ago, when I started my career as a hairdresser, I worked for a woman who exemplified that lesson. Whenever she came to work in a bad mood, her energies hit me as soon as I walked into the salon. Every time I felt those energies, I knew it would be a tough day. My boss usually kept herself from lashing out, but her negative energies remained. Even our clients could feel them: as I shampooed their hair, they'd often ask me, "What's up with her today?" Just one person's energies affected the whole salon. Where did that negativity go when we left work? Did I take it home with me? Did others? Who had a bad day because of her negative energies? One thing is certain: that negative energy had a ripple effect.

In my life, my intention is to stay mindful of my energy and how it may affect others. I have learned to

Awakening the Guru Within

rein in my energy when it extends too far outward and to breathe any frustration out of my physical body. My peaceful energy draws people to me: they recognize that energy as a safe place. Carrying positive energy is all the more important to me as a business owner. In the five salons where I have worked, the salon's tone has always comes from the top down. This is true of any workplace. What clients feel when they walk through the front door is the energy the owner has established, even if he or she is not working that day.

When I opened my own business, I was mindful that I had the power to set its tone. My intention was to make my business a place of peaceful, healing energies, so I named it Sanctuary by Joyce. Now, new clients come in the front door and tell me they feel better already, just from entering my space. Each time I hear that, my heart sings a little. I realize, "I have done what I set out to do." I have created a safe sanctuary, away from the chaos from the outside world.

All of us can and must examine the energies in our lives. On any given day, you are living among dozens of people and their energies. Some of their energies may empower you; others can feel bad, even toxic. It is so important to keep yourself and your energies balanced. You must be a force for good in other people's lives, as well as your own.

Joyce Fennell

To keep my energies balanced, I practice a routine that meets my needs. I drive in silence: no radio, no news, and no chaos. I need time to be with myself and process my day. I do not go home and talk on the phone all night; I usually don't even answer the phone at night unless my kids call. I usually make dinner, which is creative in nature, and helps me center myself. In the mornings, I allow myself time to sit and just be; in the summer, I love spending mornings on my front porch, watching the nature around me and feeling one with all living things. Eventually, I take another silent drive, and my workday begins.

My work is meditative in nature, so I do not have a daily meditation practice. I encourage you to find a time to meditate. Walking outside can be meditative, as can driving in silence. Painting, cooking, or listening to music can also work. You must find what works for you: it is so important to quiet the mind. The mind can twist you up sometimes, with all its thoughts and lists. Learning to shut off your mind is a gift you give yourself. Sometimes our minds talk to us in ways we would never allow from someone else. Those toxic thoughts are just garbage we need to dump. Replace them with pure, loving thoughts.

Whether we are talking to ourselves or to others, our words have power beyond what we can imagine. Let us use our words to help, not harm. Be mindful that every thought and action has an equal or greater reaction in energies. Ask yourself: what actions and reactions are my thoughts and words creating once released into the universe?

When you get a sense of something, your energy is Awake. All your senses are picking up information from other people and from the universal energy. You may feel this information in your body; you may see beyond the things around you; you may hear, taste, or smell something. The feeling is visceral, and you may not always realize it's not yours. Your body is receiving outside information and integrating it into your physical body, causing a physical response. Often, I feel a discomfort in my body that seems random at first. Later, however, a client will come into my room with the exact same complaint. This is a visceral reaction: an emphatic sensing of information coming into my physical body before it even enters my room.

We have all come through huge energy shifts, and we have not finished yet. Mother Earth is rumbling and shaking: she is crying out for us to make changes while we can. We as a species must heed these warnings and start taking action today. Tomorrow just won't do: we no longer have the luxury of time.

Joyce Fennell

As your consciousness shifts, the consciousness of those around you will shift, too. Those who don't make the shift will fall away. If and when that happens, do not get in the way of this process. We all have to let go of people or things sometimes, as difficult as it may seem. I have grown apart from longtime friends and clients, and I try not to take it personally. However, I can't help wondering why we grew apart; sometimes I even question myself.

In truth, this change is for a higher good. I have taken these people as far as I could, and for our time together, I am grateful. If we continue to see the same people over and over again, no new energy comes in for us to support or to support us. Everyone we meet has something to teach us. We must be willing to learn, accept the lessons along the way, and not get too attached to the messenger.

Chapter 4: Working with Collective Energy

Understanding Our Energies

In my work as an energy healer, I have come to realize that energy is energy, no matter what you call it. We must work *with* these energies to achieve the best possible results on a physical, emotional, spiritual, and soul level. Imagine a world without dis-ease and discontent, where we have the ability to heal ourselves, each other, and our planet. That world already exists. If we all tap into the universe's positive, healing energies, we can bring that world to light. We all have that ability: to connect with the world around us, to spread positive energy, and to heal our world.

Your greatest Guru lives within you. You may need guidance to find and work with your Guru Within, and sometimes, spiritual teachers and healers can help you with that. Above all, however, this work is an inside job. It always has been and it always will be. No one can do the work for you: your journey and Awakening are singularly your own.

As you move forward, you will begin to see and feel the energies of all things, from friends, family, and new people you meet along the way, to a single blade of grass. Every living thing has energies and emits them in vibrations, which reflect the true nature of their being. You may think butterflies are small in stature, for instance, but their energies may vibrate sky-high. We must keep ourselves aware of other beings' energies as we navigate our paths through the world.

We are always bumping into other people's and things' energies. These interactions show us our need to acknowledge, work with, and protect our own energy fields. Above all, we must be mindful of our thoughts and words. They have power and energy beyond measure. Your words, in particular, send energy out into the universe and affect the people they pass along the way. If you speak of someone negatively, you create negative energies which will ultimately reach that person, whether you realize it or not. Be mindful not to worry too much either: you may unintentionally put the energy of the thing you are worried about into

Awakening the Guru Within

motion. Instead, choose to send light, love, and protection into the world. Not only do these feelings spread positive energies, but they bring positive energies back to you as well. Energy is like a boomerang: you send it out and eventually, it will come back to you.

I realize some of these concepts may be new to you. Imagine a bouquet of balloons bumping into each other: these balloons are our energies, constantly colliding. Now, imagine that with every thought, action, or words you speak, a balloon floats away from the bunch. Who knows where the balloon will fly or land? Who knows how that balloon will affect everyone who sees it, everyone it touches? Be mindful of the balloons you inflate and release. Your thoughts and words can soar farther than you ever imagined.

Send someone light and love and see how their day unfolds. Have them send light and love back to you. See how people begin to respond differently: negative feelings will not stick to you, and people with positive outlooks will be drawn into your life.

Every moment of our lives, we are gathering information from the energies around us. The energies of chaos and disorder, of peace and contentment — they are drawn to each other like magnets. Surrounding yourself with chaos will bring the energy of chaos into your mind, body, and spirit. Once connected, these vibrations will require tremendous effort to break apart.

When you align yourself with the vibrations of light and love, you will impact the world in a positive way. I realize the world's problems may seem too big to shift; people and policies seem entrenched in terror and hate. However, each one of us can choose to spread light, love, and healing energies. Do something good in your community: your goodness will inspire someone else to do good as well. Good deeds inspire other good deeds. This is how we can improve our world, one act of goodness at a time. When you turn your light on, you will inspire others to turn their light on as well. As long as we choose light over darkness, we will spread light, person by person. Through this process, we will illuminate and elevate our world, together.

I had an 'aha' moment the other day while driving to work, thinking about the part of the Bible when Jesus says, "Where two or three gather in my name, I am with them" (Matthew 18:20). I realized this statement refers to energy. When we gather together for a higher purpose, we unify in divine, universal energy. We can use this energy to carry out the higher powers' work, bringing goodness and light to all we do. Or, if we make different choices, we may create negative, harmful situations instead.

Have you ever heard of John of God? He is a healer in Brazil, sought out by people all over the world. Immediately after his healing sessions with you, you sit in a room with other participants, praying and meditating for as long as he recommends for your healing — hours or even days. Similarly, in Cleveland, Dr. Issam Nemeh conducts healing sessions in churches, while the pews are full of people. Both John of God and Dr. Nemeh carry a central principle: the power of people's prayer and their intentions. When people work together, on healing or anything else, their collective energy is more powerful than that of a single source. When we work together toward a common goal, embracing all we are and all we can be, our journey goes faster and gives us more experiences and opportunities.

You will still confront insecurities and doubts; you will still stumble at times. When you do, remember that you are still learning: no one hits a home run their first time at bat. Fulfilling your purpose, like anything, is a process, and the more you open up to your journey, the more your journey will open up to you. Be Awake enough in your life to bring your best self forward, for the good of yourself, your families, your neighbors, and future generations.

Choosing Light over Darkness

We must never dim our own lights to allow another person's lights shine more brightly. Indeed, that way of thinking — that your light must come at another's expense — is incorrect. Light attracts light: when your light shines, others' lights will shine, too. Think of a row of candles: when you light one candle, its flame spreads from wick to wick. Eventually, light fills the entire room, illuminating every corner and crevice, even dark areas we would not see otherwise. Lighting the darkness, one candle at a time.

During this process, you must keep in mind: just as light attracts light, darkness attracts darkness. We must take responsibility for our actions and choose goodness and light, even when tempted to act in harmful ways. Your friends may invite you to gossip about or poke fun at someone; you may feel uncomfortable intervening when you see bullying. When you choose to stay passive, your light does not go out instantly. It just dims more and more with each passing moment. All of a sudden, you will find yourself in the dark, wondering how you got there.

Awakening the Guru Within

This spiritual law applies to everyone who commits bad acts, no matter their reasons for doing so. The cycle of abuse is a clear example of darkness breeding darkness. We must show compassion to those who have suffered at others' hands. We must listen to and acknowledge their stories, help them seek therapy, hold them up when they need us, and let go when they are ready. However, part of supporting others is encouraging them to act in kindness and goodness, always. We disempower people when we allow and ignore their bad acts. Experiencing abuse does not excuse a person's bad acts.

Please, do not condemn yourself if you act badly or slip into darkness. We all stumble sometimes: making mistakes is as human as breathing. You must know how to begin again — how to turn your light back on. First, take responsibility for your choices and apologize to the people you have harmed. Think of the lessons you have learned from your experience and keep them in your mind. Then, act with intention. Be kind, considerate, loving, and nurturing toward everyone around you. Think before you act and react. Keep taking responsibility for the choices you make. As you continue committing good deeds, soon, you will become a beacon of light again. That power to spread goodness and light starts in your choice.

Joyce Fennell

Create and embrace collective energies which help, rather than harm, you and the people around you. Think of the collective energy of riots. Riots begin when one person acts out of a chaotic, aggressive energy, which spreads to more and more people. Eventually, this chaotic, aggressive energy become the riot's collective energy, to the detriment of most people involved. In contrast, think of a candlelight vigil. There, the collective energy spreads light and love amid darkness, providing healing and sanctuary to everyone present. We must choose to create and embrace these latter collective energies — energies which elevate us, our fellow human beings, and the world.

Choose to be a beacon of light, always. Ask the divine energies to fill you with the universe's love and light. Allow that energy to flood you: every cell, organ, and system of your body, every space within your mind, body, spirit, and soul. Ask to bathe every part of yourself with the light and love of source's divine energy, the most powerful energy in the universe. Receive it in every part of yourself with gratitude. Breathe it in through your nose, mouth, and skin. Feel this energy enter through the top of your head, your crown chakra, and through your hands and feet. This life force is all that is, filling every part of you with the most powerful, loving light you could ever imagine.

Feel your senses begin to Awaken and feel warmth and peace throughout your being. Feel at one with all living, breathing beings and all spirits surrounding us. Feel at one with the divine consciousness who granted you this gift. You are part of something greater than yourself and your world. You are present with everything that is.

Spread this light with all you encounter in life. There is nothing specific you must do or say. Go out with the intention of spreading this light and love to everyone you meet. Know that you will impact everyone and everything you touch in a positive way. Then, they will impact all they touch in a positive way as well. This is how we create change, right here, right now, moving our world toward the light.

We are all energetic beings, magnificent and majestic, full of hope, promise, and life force energy. Affirm out loud: "Only light and love come through me and to me, then out into our world."

Following Your Bliss

As energetic beings, we come into this world directly from the source. It does not matter what body you reside in: tall or short, large or small build, blonde or brunette, twenty or sixty. It does not matter if you work as a janitor or as a CEO, or if you do not work at all. When we take our first breaths, we do not just breathe in air: we breathe in energy, too, in the form of our souls. Our souls make us who we are and give us the blueprints for our lives. They chose their paths — our paths — before they chose to enter our physical bodies. With free will, we can choose how to follow these paths. However, we have already agreed *to* fulfill our destinies, before we came into our bodies.

You also have the free will to choose whether to serve others or yourself. This is not to say that one decision will dictate your actions for the rest of your life. These choices happen over time, with each and every decision you make along the way. Think of a neighborhood baseball game: you can either pick the best players to win every time, or you can pick the worst player first — the one who's always picked last — and make them feel valued. You may still win the game that day, as a reward from the higher powers for your goodness. Even if you do not win the game, however, you will have shifted your energy from self-serving egotism to light, serving the people around you.

Yet you must still make choices which help you fulfill your destiny. For instance, you can choose the career which makes you the most money, or you can choose to follow your bliss. Which of these paths leads you to a higher state of enlightenment? The answer is almost always the latter. I advise you to follow your bliss and, as it evolves, to follow your new bliss as well. When you do what you love, the energy of abundance will support you. Be mindful of how you are earning money. Money is just energy, neither good nor evil. Some people, such as philanthropists, can even use their money to help others. But you must remember the duality of money. Despite its usefulness, money will never bring you true joy. Be intentional with the energy of abundance you have. Use it carefully, in pursuit of the greatest good.

That pursuit often requires you to clear yourself of negative energies. First, cleanse and clear yourself, your home, and your workplace. You may use a smudge stick, sage spray, sweet grass, or ask someone to come and cleanse the space for you. You could also ask someone do to a house blessing: this can purify any space. Eventually, as you move forward, your energetic frequency will rise, and the frequencies of those around you may rise as well. This shift does not happen by osmosis: you must act to change energies within yourself, and the energies of others will shift around you.

Allow yourself to feel the divine energies and life force within you. Receive your own power. Know that you can and will change the parts of your life that you need to change. Begin by affirming yourself. Take a few moments to settle into a comfortable place. Say the affirmations below, and you can add your own. Use only positive, "I am" statements, which empower your potential. Now, take a few, relaxing breaths, and say aloud:

"*I affirm that* I am powerful beyond measure."

"I am magnificent, beautiful, and majestic."

"I am the change I want to see in the world."

"I am a peaceful, nurturing being."

"I am living a purposeful life."

"I am the pure light and love of divine consciousness."

"I am following my guidance."

"I am in gratitude for all I have received and created."

"I am in gratitude for the Awakened being I am becoming."

Use these affirmations as often as you like, repeating them nine times each aloud. Add or exclude anything you need to along the way. Over time, you will change these affirmations because of the changes within yourself.

Awakening the Guru Within

Consider the energy you are present in now, the energy within you, and the energy you are radiating. Do your thoughts and energies match up with where you want to go and what you are creating? Realize that not every thought that enters your head is true or authentic to your being. Sometimes, thoughts just pop into your mind, whether you welcome them or not. When that happens to me, I recognize those thoughts are not my own. I am just picking up on some energy that has nothing to do with me, and I push those inauthentic thoughts out of my head. I have practiced assessing these thoughts: it takes time to learn how to recognize these messages in your own mind. Sometimes the best reaction to a thought is to stop and say, "Hmm, isn't that interesting?" and wait for further instruction or information. Believe me, if that thought is yours, its message will reappear more and more clearly every time.

As you recognize your own thoughts, you can take action on them. However, I think it is important not to act too much on impulse. Check in with your physical body first. How does this action feel in your body? Does it make you feel excitement and joy, or does it make you feel a sense of dread? Do not lose sight of the physical, emotional, and spiritual messages you are receiving while you are evaluating the message that

Joyce Fennell

you are receiving. Incorporate that information into your life and make the choice which will lead you closer to your destiny.

Using Your Past to Create Your Future

Whatever experiences you have had before now were dress rehearsals for what comes next. All those experiences taught you something — even if you wish those lessons were things you did not have to learn. Welcome or not, these lessons have helped you become who and what you are. Some of us — myself included — spend our entire lives learning. Be grateful for all your lessons. Take the lead: share what you have learned with whoever will listen.

Think of your energy in terms of sales. Do you want to be the person who is so desperate for a sale that they get right in the customer's face? These people are pushy, almost bullying. They drive customers away from them. Or do you want to be a different kind of salesperson, one who gives the customer just enough information and walks away? This second salesperson allows the customer consider the information she gave them so that later, they may come back and want to learn more about her product or service. That is energy in motion. Do you want to spread pushy, bullying energy, moving people away from you? Or do you want to respect people's energies and invite them to come back to you to learn more? I opt for the second option. What kind of energy do you want to put into the world? That is a choice we make each and every day.

Use this exercise to understand the different energies people put into the world. I put up photos, side-by-side, of two people with completely different energies. I tend to choose pairs familiar to us, like Luke Skywalker/Darth Vader and Harry Potter/Lord Voldemort. Some are complete opposites and some are not as obvious. You can do this exercise with famous people or with people in your own life. Once you have put up your photos, you can choose whether to keep your eyes open or to close them. Then, ask yourself:

"How does each person feel to me, energetically?"

"Do these people have integrity?"

"Which person has positive energy?"

"Is this person trustworthy?"

"Which person has real power energetically?"

"Who resonates with me?"

"Who is vibrating good energies?"

"What is this person's energy projecting into the world?"

Joyce Fennell

Feel these people's energies in your physical body. Allow your logical, conditioned mind to fall away. As you conduct this exercise, you will begin to feel the differences in these people's energies. Once you gain practice with this exercise, you will be able to apply this way of accessing energy to people in your own life as well. You will learn whose energies you want to be around, whose match yours and whose do not. You will learn who to move close to and who to move away from.

You will also learn what changes you need to make in your own life to attract positive energies. If you desire financial abundance, do not complain about being broke: a mindset of lack brings you more lack. Instead, change your mindset, putting out the vibrations of having the abundance you seek. When the energy you radiate meets the vibrations of that which you desire, you will receive the thing you want. That is the spiritual law. The same is true for people: if you want to attract a person with certain energy, put vibrations of the same energy into the world. Eventually, you will bring people into your life whose energies match your own.

Chapter 5: Embracing the Universal Energy

The Universal Energy

There is one universal energy. Everyone and everything is part of it. Imagine this energy is like a spider's web, individual strands spun together to make one solid structure — a home. See humanity supported within this web of life, with spirits, guides, and angels holding it up. Feel the divine energy in and around the web, from top to bottom. We all have individual purposes as well as a collective purpose. We can no longer walk this earth and live in our own little world. We can no longer think our lives and choices only affect ourselves.

We as a collective energy must find a way to work together to create a better tomorrow. This work is already happening, whether you acknowledge it or not. Every action you take causes an equal reaction, be it good, bad, or indifferent, even if it does not happen in your presence. This is how energy in motion works. Think of dropping a pebble into a lake, creating ripples in the water. Your action — dropping a pebble — causes ripples whether you pay attention or not. The ripples continue, going farther and farther in the water, even if you cannot see them from where you're standing. Eventually, those ripples bump into the shore on the other side of the lake. Our energy works the same way: part of an inevitable cause-and-effect.

The energies are vibrating from the divine universal energy, that web of life that supports all of humanity. To embrace this divine universal energy, begin with some of these simple exercises. You may do some of these already. If so, continue them or ramp them up.

Detoxify your mind, body, and spirit.
Spend time in nature.
Embrace massages, energy healing, and yoga.
Practice meditation, prayer, and journaling.
Begin daily rituals of cleansing and purification.
Find a community of like-minded people.
Block out outside influence.

These exercises work in sync with each other — and they can come easily to you, or be very challenging.

Either way, they will allow you to stretch farther than you have ever stretched before. Let me explain them in more detail.

1. Detoxify Your Mind, Body, and Spirit

When I think about detoxifying my mind, body, and spirit, I realize I must do four things: listen, read, embrace stillness, and plant seeds.

To *listen*, turn off your devices — anything bringing others' images, voices, and noises into your mind. Be still and feel the silence within your body. From this place of silence, you can listen to the things you need to hear. Listen to your own thoughts first. Sift through them to find the positive thoughts, pushing negative ones out of your mind. Listen to the sounds of nature: birds singing, winds blowing, ocean waves crashing against the shore. Listen for the sounds of your environment: dogs barking, horns honking, distant conversations. Start listening to all the sounds around you, all the time. Your brain spends so much time processing electronic noises from your phones, TVs, and computers. It's no wonder you don't hear nature or your own thoughts anymore. Stop letting devices' meaningless noises block out the things you need to hear. It's time to start listening to yourself and the world around you, maybe for the first time in your life.

Joyce Fennell

Be present with the listening: there is so much information for you to discover.

When you *read*, choose nonviolent, positive materials that feed your mind and spirit. A lot of negative energy comes from news sources and gossip magazines. Think for a moment about how these publications get you worked up. Recognize the negative energies these sources create, individually and collectively. Instead of receiving these negative energies, find materials that feed the peace within yourself. Read the works of great spiritual minds. Find authors whose writings bring you joy and empower you. When you fill your mind with goodness and light through such work, you will translate that positivity into your actions. Garbage in, garbage out; goodness in, goodness out. Allow the goodness in, so you can give goodness back to others.

You must also *embrace stillness*. Be still and quiet, bringing your attention to the deepest parts of yourself. You will find a peaceful stillness, a sense of nothingness, there — nothing to do or be. This stillness will speak to you if you are listening. Small changes to your daily routine can help you hear your stillness more clearly. I drive in silence, to process the day and receive insight from the peace inside myself. You can also change the sound of your morning alarm from a foul, blaring noise, such as barking or honking, to

Awakening the Guru Within

something more peaceful. Choose a sound that resonates with you — church bells or music, perhaps, or even birdsong. This one change can make a noticeable, positive impact in your life. Start setting the tone for your day when you wake up.

These steps — listening, reading, and embracing stillness — become part of *planting seeds*. Those seeds are your thoughts; the garden is your mind. Do you see weeds among your flowers? Treat this garden the way you would treat a real one:

Pull out the weeds: Identify and get rid of any negative energies that are choking off the energy of your growth.

Turn over the soil: Clear out the old, negative emotions and ideas from your life. Expose the new, positive energies at work, deep within yourself.

Feed the soil: Feed your mind, body, spirit and soul with positive influences such as books, music, nature sounds, meditation, and prayer.

Rake the soil: Fine-tune your daily rituals. Be mindful of what you are spending your energy doing.

Envision your garden: Have a vision of the life you are creating. See your life transforming in as much detail as you can. Imagine it in your mind's eye.

Sow your seeds: Choose the energies you are planting and creating with intention.

Nurture your plants: Read, write, and pray. Be the light you are here to be.

Keep pulling out weeds: You will keep finding negativity in your mind. Dig it out. Do not let negative energies take root within you.

Watch your garden grow: See and feel your life working in a new way. Be in gratitude for the gifts you have received and will continue to receive. Be a witness your own life, the magical transformation and growth that is happening, and how beautiful your garden is. Feel your garden's energy: it is full of life, peace, hope, joy, and possibilities. It is magical and mystical.

2. *Spend Time in and Be Nurtured by Nature*

Allow nature to embrace and inspire you. Take a walk in the park, in the mountains, at the beach, or even in your own neighborhood. Get outside as much as possible. Be present with nature along the way: please do not to wear ear buds or use your cell phone. Look at the plants and animals around you. Notice the colors of leaves and flowers. Listen to binds sing and leaves rustle. See and hear water running. Feel the ground beneath you, be it grass, dirt, sand, stone, or cement. Feel the breeze on your skin. Breathe in the fresh air. Pause for moments. Sit in the grass or on the sand; take your shoes off. Stop moving and start listening. Draw the energy of Mother Earth into your body and feel it energize you. Acknowledge that the earth lives and breathes, just like you do. Awaken to nature's energies and feel them in the core of your being. Let Mother Earth nurture you, and experience her fully in every moment. Her energy is all-powerful, life-giving, and life-sustaining.

If you think you are too busy to spend this time in nature, or you find that idea too boring, you need nature most of all. Ask yourself: why can't you ever stop? Why isn't it okay to spend time in nature, silent and present with the world around you? We have spent too long living unconsciously, as individuals and as a society, like hamsters running in a wheel. You are standing on an edge, ready to Awaken the sleeping giant within you. What feels right for you as you seek your destiny and purpose? Listen to your Guru Within. Block out the voices of naysayers who have not heard your soul's calling. All your hopes, wishes, and dreams are within you, placed there by your soul's commitment to doing and being all you came here to do and be. You have more power than you know: once you tap into the energies inside you, you can accomplish whatever you dream. Embrace your soul's calling and take action to fulfill your destiny.

3. Embrace Massages, Energy Healing, and Yoga

When we pursue spiritual Awakening, we must not ignore the physical bodies our spirits reside in. Our bodies hold all the information we need to achieve holistic success in our lives. Too often, we treat our bodies as a dump for our garbage, all the negativity we encounter. We keep shoveling trash into the heap and compacting it so we can dump in even more. Have you ever seen a garbage dump? It's hideous: piled full of trash so high, you can't see the ground anymore; pipes sticking out of the mounds of garbage, releasing toxic gasses into the air. By mishandling the negativity in our lives, we turn our bodies into garbage dumps like these, physically and metaphysically. We must get rid of this garbage and the toxicity it carries.

To do that, we have to get physical. I do not believe we need to dig up and sift through all our negative experiences to release them. However, we must recognize that negativity exists within us and can be causing us harm. We all have the power to acknowledge and release this negativity from our bodies. Are you ready to release the old thoughts, ideas, memories, and emotions that are keeping you stuck? We can heal our souls by healing our bodies. You may need experienced practitioners to help you with this work: take your time to find the individuals who best meet your needs. Once you find them, you can engage in physical treatments such as massage therapy, energy healing, and yoga, which will help you move your energies forward. *The Healing Code*, a powerful book by Alexander Loyd and Ben Johnson, may help you as well.

Massage therapy can help release stress in your body like nothing else. It also helps remove blocks in energy and movement, relieving old pain patterns and creating new muscle memory. By moving energy, blood, and life force through your body, massage therapy can give you physical, emotional, and spiritual clarity. With that, you can become a clear channel in your own life, modeling to those around you what their best lives can look and feel like as well. Your newly healthy physical body will help you complete the task at hand: fulfilling your destiny and purpose.

Energy healing can come in different forms. Reiki, polarity, craniosacral therapy, reconnective healing, acupuncture, and therapeutic touch are just a few examples. In any of these practices, the chi, or life force, must move in a free, balanced way for optimal health and wellbeing. Imagine the energy in your body is like water running through a hose: if you get a clump of mud in the hose, the water can't pass through it. These energy blocks can be physical, emotional, or spiritual;

they make you feel uncomfortable and stagnant. Energy healing helps you remove these blocks so your energy can flow freely through your body, for optimal health and wellness in your mind, body, spirit and soul.

Yoga creates an opening of energy in your physical, emotional, and spiritual bodies. By incorporating movement and meditation together, in sync, yoga becomes a physical as well as a spiritual practice. When you experience an energy block, yoga can help by stirring your energies, loosening the block, and moving it out of your mind, body, spirit, and soul. Because you can practice yoga without a professional's help, a regular yoga practice can provide a useful way to regulate your energies on a daily basis. I recommend a traditional yoga practice — authentic, not trendy, such as hot yoga. Practice yoga as it was intended from its inception. If this kind of yoga does not resonate with you, look into qigong or tai chi, which also put energy in motion.

Any and all of these physical practices can help you get rid of your toxic energies. Be present and embrace the changes as they occur. Let your body, mind, and spirit unwind and release as quickly or as slowly as necessary. Do not let anyone get in your way: this process is yours, and there is no right or wrong. Be in gratitude for the lessons you have learned along the way, and then let these energies go. Finally and forever, you are getting rid of the messages and patterns that no longer serve you. You will know when you have moved through these energy blocks. You will feel healing on every level; you will feel lighter, brighter, and more hopeful. Finally at peace. Be patient with this process, as it happens in divine order. Trust the process, trust yourself, and trust the higher powers.

4. *Practice Meditation, Prayer, and Journaling*

In order to recognize the voice of the divine, your heart's desire, and your soul's destiny, you must quiet your mind. Quieting your mind is the first step of *meditation*. To begin, you need to realize that certain things we do are meditative in nature, such as taking a walk or driving your car. Embrace the stillness in these actions and listen closely to what you are hearing. Eventually, you may want to practice traditional meditation. Find a quiet place where no one will disturb you. Sit in a relaxed position, close your eyes, and begin listening to the inner dialogue in your mind. The more still and quiet your body becomes, the more still and quiet your mind will become. You will access the peace and stillness within you.

Joyce Fennell

When thoughts arise, allow these thoughts to drift out of your conscious mind. If they persist, stop and write them down and continue. Visualize your mind's eye as a blank sheet of paper, with nothing to do or be. Imagine purging your mind of any and all thoughts. This purging will take patience and practice. If you cannot quiet your mind, you just need to keep practicing, even if it feels uncomfortable. You may want to join a meditation class or pick up a CD or DVD that helps you quiet the mind through music or sound. Do whatever works for you. Sometimes the most challenging thing to do or think about is nothing, but that can also be your most powerful tool. Nothingness is the key that unlocks the information you seek. This is the power to just *be*. It Awakens you on every level.

Begin with short meditations. If you meditate too long without success, you will get frustrated. Five to fifteen minutes at first is plenty. You will begin to feel a great sense of internal peace. You will feel a oneness with your soul, the higher powers, nature, and all life forms, physical and spiritual. You will begin to Awaken parts of yourself that you may not have recognized or known before. Pay attention to these revelations and to all other information you receive. You may notice recurring, negative messages such as "You're not good enough" or "You can't do this." You may not have realized these messages lived in your subconscious, simmering beneath your conscious mind. When you recognize these messages, you can change them. Do not judge yourself or the messages: just acknowledge and release them with gratitude. This release may take some time; you may have to release them over and over again. One day, however, you will not hear these negative messages anymore, and they will no longer have power over you. By letting those old messages go, you will make room to hear new, positive messages. You will witness the new, more Awakened self emerge as the old you falls away.

Prayer is a form of meditation, allowing us access the most magnificent energies of love in the universe. I'm not talking about traditional prayers: I'm talking about conversations directly with the divine energies, whatever or whoever those are for you. These powers are the source of life and all eternity; they are all-knowing, all-powerful, and most importantly, all-loving. Their energies spread peace, harmony, and love that envelop your mind, body, spirit, and soul in an indescribable way. Your connection with these energies will be magical, mystical, majestic, and intimate all at once. Let this light and love fill you when you feel lost, empty, sad, or defeated. Allow yourself to embrace these energies of light and love, even if your logical mind cannot understand them fully.

Begin a conversation with your higher powers. As a first step, you might express gratitude for all that is working in your life. You could also express gratitude for the things that are not working, and the opportunity for growth that may come from them. Ask for guidance, direction, and clarity. Ask about your purpose and destiny. Do not ask for material things: we must not waste time focusing on mere objects. You may ask for clarification about the direction in which you are going, or about life steps such as education, jobs, or a new home. Keep the dialogue open. You are creating a relationship with your higher powers, and relationships are built over time. Be mindful of that.

The higher powers will answer you in different ways. You may suddenly have an 'aha' moment, or you may receive wisdom from someone else — a loved one or a chance encounter. You may see a street sign, a license plate, a billboard, or even a book title that tells you what you need to know. You may hear a song on the radio or see something on the TV; you may receive an opportunity or an invitation. However, you must be awake enough in your life to receive these messages. As you begin to take action based on the information you receive, more information will come in, and the

Awakening the Guru Within

message will be bigger, louder, and more powerful than ever before.

Prayer is a powerful tool, known to heal the sick and even bring people back from the brink of death. Prayer allows those of us here on earth to connect to something much greater than ourselves. You will begin to move into a more peaceful, authentic existence with confidence and the absence of fear. As your life begins to work on a larger, deeper, more purposeful level, do not abandon your conversation with the higher powers or your gratitude for all you are receiving. Keep talking to your higher powers and receiving their divine guidance and blessing.

Journaling can work in tandem with meditation and prayer. Begin to keep a record of the messages you receive so you may process them fully, gleaning every bit of wisdom from the information the higher powers are giving you. First, you must recognize what is important enough to record, even if it doesn't seem that important as you receive it. Some information comes in snippets, not all at once: you must have a record of your messages so you can paste these snippets together. By recording this information, you will begin to see how messages from the higher powers' divine energy merge with events in your life. You will also start to process this information through your creative, psychic mind. Consider writing by hand, perhaps in cursive, as studies have shown this expands your creativity by activating more neurons in your brain. Use your words to describe all you know, feel, see, taste, hear, and smell. These sensations become clearer the more you write about them, allowing you to discover things about yourself which may enlighten and surprise you.

Writing will connect you to a deeper part of yourself and the universal life force. This connection can heal and empower you; it can Awaken parts you which have been asleep for a long time, perhaps a lifetime, until now. Writing may even reveal deep truths within yourself. Why you are here? What is your purpose, your passion, your true calling, and your work in this lifetime? With each page you write, you will reveal more and more to yourself, about yourself — your most authentic self. Be intentional with your writing. Each time you write, set an intention for what you want to learn or reveal. When you ask for that revelation, the higher powers are likely to grant it. Keep writing and the answers will come. When you take action on those answers, you will begin living a more purposeful and fulfilling life. You will be able to look at your past journal entries, even when you feel stagnant energy, and see how far you have come.

Awakening the Guru Within

At times, the road ahead of you looks long. When your journey feels daunting, turn around and see how far you have come. Move forward from that place, one foot in front of the other. Your timing is divinely guided.

5. Begin Daily Rituals of Cleansing and Purification

Think of how you treat your car. Would you put bad gas in your tank? Skip oil changes? Drive on a flat? Go miles without gas? These questions may seem absurd: we care about our cars, so we would never so blatantly mistreat them. Yet we abuse our bodies every day — by eating poorly, not sleeping enough, and not drinking enough water. We have become addicted to caffeine and sugar to keep our energies up. We work until we feel exhausted and empty. We buy into this way of life and expect our bodies to keep going with no negative consequences.

Eventually, we will hit a wall: we can only keep living like this, unconscious and unhealthy, for so long. Begin treating your body as a temple instead. Keep your foods simple, without too much caffeine, sugar, artificial sweetener, food coloring, or alcohol. Keep water with you so you can hydrate yourself. Keep yourself clean and groomed daily. Keep your hair, skin, nails, teeth, and clothes clean and neat. De-clutter your home and workspace. Keep them tidy, with space for energies to flow around and through you. Surrounding yourself with too much chaos and disorder creates chaos and disorder in your mind. Chaos and disorder can then lead to discontent — physically, emotionally, and spiritually.

As you begin living in these new, healthier ways, you will make better, more conscious choices. You will begin to feel lighter, freer, happier, healthier, and wiser. As your health improves, your life will improve as well. All you have to do is wake up from your unconscious state and choose to start living a purposeful, conscious life.

6. *Find a Community of Like-Minded People*

As I've said before, fulfilling your purpose and destiny is an inside job. It always has been and it always will be. However, we live among other people and their energies. We are social beings, and we need connections with each other to live a good life. Being mindful of the people in our communities is an important part of achieving the lives we are here to live. Your community should include people who resonate with you, who share your values and can support you on your journey.

Awakening the Guru Within

Begin finding these people by putting yourself into the world in a whole new way. Look for meditation groups, yoga classes, book clubs, or other groups of people who share your interests. Ask your energy worker, yoga instructor, or therapist for recommendations. Read metaphysical and spiritual publications. Take a class in metaphysics, meditation, healing, or dream work — anything that resonates with you. When you find groups that share your interests, put yourself in a space with them. You may be drawn to some of these groups and turned off by others. Trust yourself and your instincts: if something gives you a bad vibe, walk away. We can no longer afford to be in the company of those whose motives are not pure light. Look to the people who resonate with you. Let the information you are receiving be your guide.

You will have to leave your comfort zone a little. Your current friends can only bring you so far. Be patient with the process of finding your community. You may make choices that do not turn out how you expected. Those choices can still lead you in the right direction. For instance, one of your new friendships may not be in line with your energy — but that person may introduce you to someone who will become a lifelong friend. Sometimes, people can teach you what you *don't* want in a community, too. This information is just as valuable as figuring out what you do want.

I meet people all the time who have information to share with me, even just a nugget. Sometimes, they stay in my community for years; other times, just for a moment. Finding your community is a lifelong process. Grant yourself patience as new people, interests, and values enter your life. You may never stop building your community, but that process will only bring more loving energies into your life.

7. *Block Out Outside Influences*

We receive so much outside stimulation, especially from electronic devices. When we receive a call, email, or text message, we feel we must answer them immediately, or at least check who sent them. These small forces have huge impacts in our lives. According to a University of California, Irvine study, it takes almost half an hour, on average, to return to our original tasks after such interruptions. When we keep Facebook, Twitter, Instagram, and Snapchat accounts, we feel we have to log on at least once a day. We don't want to miss anything. Televisions and radios take up our time and energies as well. We become so involved in other people's stories that we neglect to write our own.

Awakening the Guru Within

This addiction to technology is a cultural ailment. Next time you go to a restaurant, look around: more than half the customers are probably looking at their phones. However, we have the power to cure ourselves of this problem. We must choose to disconnect. Turn off your devices and put them away: out of sight, out of mind. Make conscious efforts to keep your devices at home or, at the very least, in your pockets. Notice how you connect with the world around you without a screen as your intermediary. You will find more beauty and opportunities. You will meet more people who can bring light and love into your world.

I encourage you to power down daily. Without technology's influence, your mind will de-clutter and expand to embrace every part of your journey. Affirm out loud:

"I choose to power down at this time, so I may hear my own thoughts. This will enable me to connect with my higher self, my soul self, in order to move my life in the direction of my dreams, desires, and destiny. I am open to receiving all the information available to me in these moments. I commit to being present in each moment, the moment I am in it."

Work with this process of powering down to access your highest, best life. Choose every day to allow this process to open up your heart, mind and soul, in

Joyce Fennell

unimaginable ways. What you discover along the way may be surprising, even magical.

Chapter 6: Living With Intention

Setting Your Intentions

Set your intentions to manifest the life you desire. Begin by thinking about the direction in which you are going. What is tugging at your heart? What is speaking loudly to you, trying to get your attention? Identifying this desire is a good first step in creating your must abundant, authentic life. Consider the changes you would like to make, too. What are your hopes, wishes, and dreams right now? What are your hopes, wishes, and dreams for the future? Be mindful and reflective. Ask for direction in prayer. Remember that you are co-creating your life with the divine energies: you are ready to receive what you are asking for. Imagine creating your most authentic, abundant life, the life you are here to live, and becoming who you are here to be.

Once you are ready to set your intentions, put pen to paper and write them, letting ideas stream out of your consciousness. Rewrite the intentions once you have finished. I recommend using "I am" statements: they carry powerful, positive energy. Avoid phrases such as "I will try," which implies you will not succeed; "I want," which creates more wants; or "I should," which judges yourself and others. You must only write positive, nonjudgmental intentions.

Using mindful language is important as well. One time, when I was trying to lose weight, I started every day by saying out loud, "I am losing weight with little to no effort in a healthy way," and the pounds melted off. Sounds great, right? However, my intention had the wrong focus: I intended to lose weight, not to become my healthiest weight. As a result, I gained back the weight I had lost, and then I had more weight to lose. My story shows you must be mindful of the words you choose, because energies attract matching energies: it is spiritual law. Your words go out as energy and boomerang back to you, bringing with them the energy of whatever you have asked for, whether you asked for it consciously or not. Because you have the power to achieve all your intentions, you must set exactly the

Awakening the Guru Within

intentions you desire to create. Ask for the life you desire on every level, with no limitations.

People's intentions vary depending on their lives and the lives they are here to live. However, we can still discuss some common intentions, based on desires many people share. These intentions may include:

"I am living a peaceful, joyful life."

"I am one with nature and the higher powers' divine energy."

"I am receiving light and love."

"I am radiating light and love in all I do."

"I am free to live my authentic life."

"I am surrounded by like-minded people."

"I am working in a job I love."

"I am healthy physically, emotionally, and spiritually."

"I am living an abundant life in all areas."

"I am in healthy, strong relationships."

"I am pure light and love."

"I am present in my life for myself and for those around me."

"I am following my guidance."

"I am grateful."

Once you write your intentions, read them aloud and check in with your physical body. How do your intentions make you feel? Do they make you feel alive, inspired, joyful, and hopeful in the core of your being? If they do not, you may want to remove any intentions that feel too heavy for now. This is an ongoing process: you can add or remove intentions anytime as long as they lead you where you want to go.

However, writing your intentions is not enough: you must also work with them. Read your intentions in a ritual every morning, every evening, and other times a day. Voicing your intentions gives them more energy and power. Keep a few copies of them: one at home, one in your car, and one at work. Read your intentions when you see them throughout the day and read them right before you go to sleep. This practice can lead to some powerful changes. As you read your intentions, you will hear them as well. You may want to choose one item on the list and make it your main focus for the day. Repeat your intention often and live in pursuit of it from sunup to sundown. See what happens. As you work with and reflect upon your intentions, you will start to receive what you have asked for. Watch your life begin to flow toward the life you are here to live.

Transforming Your Life

Align yourself with the life you are creating all day, every day. Be intentional with the words you say, the

Awakening the Guru Within

thoughts you have, the people you meet, and the food and drink you choose. Be mindful of the way you work and move your body. Be mindful of what you read, what you watch on TV, and who and what you listen to. Be mindful of how you react to the situations you are presented with each day, in every moment. If you want to live a more Awakened and spiritual life, you cannot restrict it to Sundays. Living that life must happen every day, in every moment, with every choice you make. Even the smallest, most mundane tasks matter.

Step outside yourself so you can observe yourself acting through this process. Ask yourself, "Where do I have the most challenges? What pushes my buttons? What comes easily? What feeds my soul? What lessons am I learning along the way?" Do not judge yourself: just recognize and acknowledge your behaviors. Otherwise, you cannot change them. All the while, remain in gratitude for every moment, person, and experience. These things make us who we are. Thank the higher powers for all the lessons you have learned and are learning. Even when life seems too difficult, be grateful you woke up that morning and got out of bed on your own two feet. That small action was your choice; that small action led you closer to your hopes, wishes and dreams. Always remember your power of choice, and choose to make each day awesome.

When in doubt about what action to take, ask yourself: "What would my higher power do?" For that matter, what would your most Awakened self do? Ask before you act. Take a moment and pause to hear the answer; acting or reacting too quickly can set you off-track. Once you have practiced this process long enough, asking before taking action will become second nature to you. Remember the importance of intention, consciousness, mindfulness, and practice in becoming a more spiritually balanced being. Be present in your life, listen to your inner guidance, and most importantly, trust yourself.

As part of that trust and presence, you must allow yourself to change when necessary. We are accumulations of all our experiences; they form our relationships, our choices, and our beliefs. However, because we constantly have new experiences, we are constantly changing. That is a good thing: with every change, we grow closer to our full, authentic selves. Think of dandelions gone to seed. Watching dandelions transform reminds us that even beautiful, vibrant things may need to change. As they dandelions die off, their seeds blow away, creating new life somewhere else. Our lives can mirror this process: we create beautiful lives for ourselves, but sometimes, parts of us must fade away so that new energies can grow in their place. Be open to this transformation and to receiving new parts of yourself. These parts will transform into something new — something even more wonderful than you could have ever imagined.

Manifesting Your Desires

If you are not manifesting the life you want, you are manifesting the life you have. We cannot grow from keeping our lives the same, small and comfortable. We all have the ability to manifest our desires, and we need to put this ability into practice. As a lifelong learner, I can say from personal experience that the resources we need to develop this ability will show up when we are ready and willing students. Over time, by using these resources — classes, books, articles, teachers who have guided me along the way — I have learned how to manifest my dreams and desires. Most of all, I have become my own guru by listening to my Guru Within. This inner voice has helped me achieve my goals, no matter what they were.

One dream I manifested was a trip to Italy. Three and a half years ago, I decided to begin manifesting that desire by acknowledging its physical requirements. I got an envelope, wrote "Italy" on the front, and drew a boot — the country's shape — underneath. For a year, I put money in the envelope to fund my trip. Then, one day, I felt divinely guided and applied for an airline credit card. I did this so I could earn miles to pay for my tickets to and from Italy. Two and a half years later, I booked my tickets, and all I had to pay was tax. I planned carefully and stayed patient with the process. Ultimately, I manifested my desire by making the choices my gut told me were right. I knew these choices would bring the energy of what I was asking for to me. By the time the trip came up, I had saved enough cash to fund the rest of the trip.

Another time that I needed to create extra money, I practiced a feng shui technique. Every day for nine days in a row, I put money in a box under my bed. I set the intention to create abundance; I believed in my ability to create abundance. For those nine days, I did not borrow the money in that box for any reason. If you use this technique, the universe will begin rewarding you with abundance either during or after those nine days. I began to receive abundance after my nine days of saving — from unexpected sources. First, I met up with a former coworker of mine who had just moved back to Cleveland from New York. She gave me a necklace made by a top designer, as a thank-you for a facial I had given her years ago. Not long afterwards, I practiced doing a complementary reconnection — a healing session — on a friend. At that time, I was still learning how to do this healing modality, and I practiced free of charge. However, my friend insisted on paying me, and although I refused at first, he gave me a check for $333.00 — the exact charge for the treatment channeled by Dr. Eric Pearl, the founder of this healing modality. Once my training was complete, I planned to charge 333.00 for the treatment as well. I thanked my friend and went on my way, grateful for that gift.

Receiving that check taught me an additional lesson: Be mindful of not rejecting the gifts that the universe gives you. Sometimes, we do not know what we will create. Every gift we receive is something we have asked for energetically, even if we expected it to come in a different form. Accept your gifts with gratitude, grace, and an open heart, no matter what form they take. If you decline these gifts, you may block the exact energies you need to move forward on your journey.

The most successful people in the world know how to manifest their dreams and desires. Did Oprah Winfrey decide her dreams were too big to follow? No. Did Mark Zuckerberg stop building Facebook when that work became difficult? People like Oprah Winfrey and Mark Zuckerberg probably never guessed how big their lives would become. However, they started manifesting their desires from where they were, not where they wanted to be. By accomplishing one goal at a time, receiving gifts from the universe with gratitude along the way, they didn't just change their lives. They changed the world.

I could share more stories about people — those you know and those you don't — manifesting their desires. You must believe in your ability to manifest your dreams and desires. One step at a time, your destiny and purpose will unfold before you. I am ready to manifest my dreams and desires, even if they seem like giant leaps from where I am now. That's what I'm doing with this book: manifesting my destiny and purpose by putting pen to paper. I have the dream and desire to teach spiritual principles and spiritual laws to those seeking deeper meaning in their lives and in the lives of those they touch. By writing this book, I am sharing all that spiritual wisdom with you.

Both Oprah Winfrey and Mark Zuckerberg have something in common with you and me: we all wake up in the morning to start our days. We all come from someplace; we all experience successes and struggles. No one is better than anyone else. We all have equal power to manifest our dreams, desires and ultimately,

Awakening the Guru Within

our destiny. Our greatness lies within reach. We just have to allow ourselves grasp it. Let's now Awaken, to all we are here to do and be, right here and right now. There is no time to waste. Now is the moment.

Chapter 7: Connecting with the Higher Powers

Opening Up to Energies

The divine energies of our higher powers are majestic and magnificent, powerful beyond measure. They are all-powerful, loving, and kind beyond what you can imagine; they radiate a light so bright and beautiful, we cannot imagine it until we receive it. These energies can help us reach our best selves, opening up to all the amazing experiences that our futures hold. Think of the bud of your favorite flower. It is tightly wound, with petals that each have their own shape, color, and size. The sun's energy cannot permeate the bud's center until it is ready. However, with the sun's help and perseverance, the flower will begin to open, one petal at a time. More petals will open with each passing day until; ultimately, the bud fully opens. At that exact time, the flower will emerge and begin to give back to the universe, adding beautiful scents and colors to its landscape. Perhaps most importantly, the flower even shares its sweet nectar, feeding and healing other beings so they may sustain life.

We humans can learn from these flowers. If we let the higher powers' divine energies open us up, we can give and receive beauty and life to everything else on the planet. We can nurture not only ourselves, but also our children, helping them grow into the people they are meant to become. Our entire world will benefit from that growth, as we begin to do and be what we are here to do and be. We must choose to open ourselves up to and connect with the higher powers' divine energies. Be brave and go willingly. Only then can we begin the lives we have only dreamed possible.

How to open ourselves up to the higher power's divine energies:

1. *Have clear intentions.*

In order to connect to the higher powers, you must commit to the process. Why do you want to commit?

Joyce Fennell

You may feel disconnected spiritually or seek deeper spiritual guidance; you may feel you need help from the higher powers to move onto the next stage in your life; you may feel that your service in this world requires a larger spiritual connection. Examine these motivations, whatever they may be. As you begin to open yourself to the higher powers and their energies, be mindful of what you are asking for and why. Are you focused on the greater good or on your own, personal greatness? What do you wish to receive? Ask for something as clear and specific as possible — something that will open up your path to Awakening and enlightenment. You may feel the love and peace of the higher powers' life force energy. You may feel connected to and supported by something that is higher than your human self. Open yourself to receiving this powerful energy. Begin sharing it with others.

2. *Prepare to accept the energy however it comes.*

The higher powers' divine energy may not come in the way you expect. However, it will come in exactly the way you need to receive it. Know that divine timing is always perfect, even if we do not understand it. Affirm to the higher powers: "I am ready to receive your divine light and guidance. I am ready to receive all that I am and will be. I trust in the process and how it shows up for me. I am willing to do the work." The higher powers will give you enough information to take the next steps on your path. Release control over this process; instead, just let it unfold. Once you get out of your own way, the higher powers will move your life forward.

3. *Ask, pray, meditate – and receive.*

Use prayer and meditation to seek guidance from the higher powers' divine energy. Ask them for guidance while you meditate; ask them for guidance while you pray and sleep. Ask the higher powers to send you guidance in a way that you can recognize and receive. Ask to become a vehicle for light and love. Ask to serve the world in a larger way. Ask for help removing your energy blocks. Quiet your mind, body, and spirit enough to hear the higher powers' answers. Affirm to them:

"I am ready to do whatever you ask of me. Please guide my steps."

"I am willing and able to receive your guidance and teaching."

"I am able to act on that guidance accordingly."

"I am in your service. Use me as a vehicle of light in our world."

Joyce Fennell

"I accept and embrace the perfect timeline for the unfolding of my spiritual being and soul self."

Accelerating this process is possible, even probable, if you spend more time working with these principles. Accept that you will receive what you need, when you need it. You may not be able to see the whole path that awaits you; you may not know what step to take right now. Trust the higher powers: your journey will unfold in divine order. The higher powers will always make the choice that is best for you. Wait for the higher powers to reveal your path; be patient and let them do their work. Once you do — once you get out of your own way — your journey will continue exactly as it should. Thank the higher powers for all that is, was, and will be. Ask to be a beacon of light for our planet.

Transition, Transformation and Transcendence

As you work through the process of opening yourself to the higher powers, you will probably go through what I call the Three T's: Transition, Transformation, and Transcendence.

A *transition* marks a time in your life when things are changing on a physical, emotional, spiritual, and even soul level. We experience transitions for most

Awakening the Guru Within

of our lives: from baby to toddler, from child to adult, from single to married, from being someone's child to being someone's parent. These are just a few examples to help you understand transitions. The higher powers constantly ask us to Awaken to new parts of ourselves when we are ready and able. These transitions can be easy or challenging depending on the person transitioning, the lessons involved, the transition itself, and what we are here to learn.

Transition is that point in time when nothing is happening and everything is happening all at once — the space between creation and manifestation. This is a time of shifts in our physical, emotional, spiritual, and soul bodies. Some shifts you may be aware of; others, you may not. Either way, the shifts are happening. We must recognize how these shifts are impacting our lives, the lives of those around us, and ultimately, the universal energy. Be mindful that you are putting positive energies into the world, no matter how much is changing in or around you. Remember: just because you cannot see something — time, energies, shifts — does not mean they are not there. Embrace these shifts for all they bring into your life, now and in the future.

Transformation follows transition. It involves a change in form, both literally and spiritually. As we transform, we change from what we were to what we will be. Pay very close attention to your thoughts and feelings during this process. Reflect on how they come in and what they reveal. At this point, the process of transformation is in its rawest form, beginning to take the shape of something new. You must stay present with this process: once you transform, you cannot go back to what you once were, energetically.

In thinking and reflecting on transformation, I am reminded of a Phil Donahue interview I saw on The Oprah Winfrey Show during her last season. Oprah had modeled her talk show after Donahue's, and at the time of interview, he had been off the air for more than a decade. In this interview, she asked him when he knew it was time to give up his talk show. His answer: when he couldn't stand to hear himself talk anymore. Essentially, Donahue was telling Oprah that he had received the higher powers' message of transformation. He completed the work he had been doing as a talk show host. He was now being called to change form, to do something new, because he had outgrown his former form. He needed to accommodate new energy coming in.

Donahue's words ring true to me: instead of listening to negative mind chatter or staying on the same path because it's comfortable, we must listen to the Guru Within and the divine energies. They will guide us to what we need to do and when we need to do it. All of us, at one point or another, will receive this divine guidance. It is the natural order of things: because we have changed, our messages change, too. Embrace the change, for what follows may be magical.

The third of the Three T's is *transcendence* — from a physical, human body to a spiritually evolved being. This does not happen for everyone. If this shift is necessary for you, it will happen; if it is not, then it will not. Not every person needs to transcend their physical body into a more ethereal body. Your most important task is to move forward in a positive way and achieve your destiny and purpose. That may not require transcendence at this time. However, in the future, you may circle back to transcendence as the next step in your journey. For now, follow your path as it is laid out: do what feels right to you. Follow your Guru Within and the higher powers' guidance, first and foremost. Regardless of whether you will transcend or not, I think it's important to know what transcendence is and that it is possible.

When you have transitioned, transformed, and you are ready to transcend, you will enter a new reality, one beyond any physical or spiritual existence you have known before. You will understand everything around you on a deeper level, even things you thought you understood. You will replace your small ideas about where you are going or what you are doing with the reality of what is truly possible, and what will happen next. Do not fear this shift into a new reality: transition and transformation have woven the net which will catch you. Once you land, you will access higher energies, transcending the physical world. You will realize new possibilities, hopes, wishes, and dreams. Without your physical and emotional limitations, you will be free to do and be what you are here to do and be. Make no mistake: both you and the universe are ready for this next step. From this elevated place, you will be ready to move toward the greater good for yourself and the world.

The journey from human to ethereal, from form to formless, is incredible. The process happens over months, even years, and each individual's process is their own. Some move through it with ease and others with some struggle. If you are meant to transcend, to move toward your destiny, you will; if it is not your time yet, you will not. However, the intention and the lessons learned will be most valuable to you moving forward into the next stage in your journey. I've said it before and I will say it again: this is an inside job. However, as you begin to transition, transform, and transcend, you will impact everything around you. The

Awakening the Guru Within

people closest to you will feel your new energy, and you will carry yourself differently in daily life. Doors will open for you, you will meet new people, and your perspective will brighten as your life changes.

Realizing the enormity of this shift is important. In some ways, you may feel that nothing has changed. In reality, however, everything has changed: your actions and reactions, from this moment onward, hold more powerful energy than ever before. You will need to be patient with yourself and this process as you learn the next steps of your path. Always remember that your guides are with you on your journey. Ask for help when you need it. Your guides and angels are there to support you — just be mindful that you must ask for their help before they can give it.

Psychic Transformation

Awakening your Guru Within is a vital way to communicate with your inner guidance. This Awakening involves being quiet and listening, working with all parts of yourself to move forward on your journey. However, we also have another way to communicate with our inner guidance: *psychic readings*. These readings, which can complement but not replace "Awakening your Guru Within", allow you to call in psychic energy and ask direct questions to the spirit world. The spirit world's guidance will help you psychically transform.

Accessing this psychic information requires a different approach than we've discussed before. Your intention in receiving this information is crucial. Remember, the intention in which you do anything is as important as what you are doing. Integrity is also essential, both for yourself and for others. You must not do a psychic reading on another person unless he or she invites you to do so: that is unethical and dishonorable. I have experienced these intrusions firsthand, forcing me to slam the door shut by stating in my mind, determined and forceful: "You are not invited." These experiences, as well as my metaphysical light worker training, taught me that psychically reading someone else without their permission feels unsettling. Committing psychic intrusion throws your energies off-balance and betrays the other person, yourself, and the divine energies' guidance. When I stopped these psychic intrusions and removed the person committing them from my life, I felt the heavy energies around me lift.

Those energies show that in psychic readings, powerful forces are at work. Always be mindful of that, and choose to operate from integrity and honor in all that you do. Be mindful, too, that this process of psychic reading happens in divine order. Life shows us what we need to know when we need to know it. The higher powers will give you this information in a way that you can receive and understand, allowing you to integrate that information into your life for the highest good. Be patient with this process, allowing divine guidance and timing. Remember that this is a new practice, and it will take exactly that — practice — for you to hear all the wisdom the spirit world can offer.

To begin this process of psychic reading, find a comfortable spot where you will not be disturbed. Sit in a comfortable position, close your eyes, and follow these steps. Take your time with this. There is no rush. Allow what needs to come in, at a pace that you can receive it.

How to conduct a psychic reading:

1. Breathe

Take some deep, cleansing breaths, in through your nose and out through your mouth. Repeat nine times. Allow a sense of relaxation to move through your whole body.

2. *Feel*

Feel the soles of your feet moving into the earth, like a tree's roots. Feel your soles grounding yourself in Mother Earth. Take a few more cleansing breaths and then begin to breathe normally again.

3. *Visualize*

In your mind's eye, visualize the top of your head receiving a golden-white light from the universe, entering through your crown chakra. Feel this powerful, loving light energy from the divine powers. Feel this energy permeate your entire physical body.

4. *See*

Bring your attention to your third eye chakra, in the center of your forehead. See and feel the opening of your third eye — your psychic eye. Take a deep, cleansing breath and exhale slowly.

5. *Welcome*

Now, welcome in the spirit world. Invite in any and all guardian angels, spiritual guides, and ascended masters who have helped you on your journey. Welcome those who wish to join you for the highest, best energies and outcomes. Ask your higher powers divine energy to be present with you now, to provide guidance and protection.

6. *Thank*

Thank all of these energies for coming in. Begin connecting with these energies. Feel them in your physical body. You may feel a tingling in your face, or an internal sense of peace. You may also feel sensations in the palms of your hands. You may want to open your hands and face them away from your body, with your palms out, to begin receiving the energies. If you are reading for another, ask them to say their name three times, and then connect your heart to theirs with an imaginary golden white cord.

7. *Ask*

It is now time to ask the questions, either for yourself or for another. Ask what you are guided to ask. Even if your questions do not make sense to you yet, ask them: the spirit world will give you answers. You can also write in a journal. Write down your questions, record what you are receiving, and write the help you need from your spiritual guides, angels, and masters.

As you acknowledge what is coming in and how it is coming in, the higher powers will reveal more and more information to you. If anything is unclear, ask for more information or clarity. If the information is coming too fast, ask the higher powers to slow down. Continue asking questions and having a conversation until you feel complete.

When you feel complete, thank the light beings and divine energies that have come in to support you. Thank them for being with you during your reading. Ask them to go in peace. Let them know that you would like to return at another time. Until then, take in some cleansing breaths as you disconnect from these energies and emerge from this psychic state, back into your physical body. Feel yourself seated where you are. Become fully present in this moment, open your eyes, and take as much time as you need before standing up. Say out loud, "I am complete with this psychic reading."

You may want to keep a journal of your readings and the information you are receiving. Know that the information will come in a way that makes sense to you. If the information does not make sense to you, it is meant for someone else. Processing this information will take some time to figure out, but the more you do it, the clearer the messages will become. You will be able to unpack and understand more and more messages and their true meanings.

Awakening the Guru Within

Let your intention be goodness and light. Let the information you receive be helpful, not harmful. Be mindful of what you are receiving and how you are receiving it. Remember, all the while, that what you do with that information is of the utmost importance.

Chapter 8: Trusting Your Inner Guidance

Sifting Through Your Thoughts

At this point, if you have been working with the processes we have discussed, you have begun experiencing a shift. Some may feel this as a gentle nudge; others, as a cosmic shift. Take time to assimilate all you have learned about your physical and spiritual life. This journey is not a race to the finish line. It is a lifelong process of opening yourself to the newest information available. Just as you are always changing, the information does, too. Bringing in new energies will be a constant in your life.

Over the past ten years, the energies of change have been supercharged. Look at our political and environmental climates! Political shifts include historic elections: in America, we went from an inclusive leader to an exclusive one, with completely opposite energies. In our environment, there has been an increase in natural disasters such as super storms, wildfires, and earthquakes — reflecting the energy shifts we've already discussed in this book.

The universe is demanding change. We, the people, have the power to co-create the new world order. This responsibility is why we must connect to the higher powers. We need their help to implement great change, to follow and spread light instead of darkness. Remember that light attracts light and darkness attracts darkness: as long as we choose light, we can heal ourselves, our planet, and the universe. When we do the work we are here to do on this earth, we live our authentic lives. We become light.

To do that work, we need to trust the guidance of our Gurus Within. We will learn to discriminate between what is just a passing thought and what is real, when to take action and when to pause. This is an exercise in trust: trusting what life is offering you and embracing all that can and will be, then moving joyfully onto the next step in your journey. I find it helpful to think of TRUST as an acronym:

Joyce Fennell

T - Truth R - Releases U - Us to S - Start   T - Trusting

Let's start small. Think of a time when someone popped into your mind — a friend you hadn't seen in weeks, perhaps. Sometimes, shortly after you think of that friend, she will reach out to you. Other times, you may reach out to her only to find something has happened in her life, and she needs your support. In these situations, your Guru Within has guided you to think of your friend. If you acted on that guidance, then you realized your friend was not just a passing thought. She needed your guidance, wisdom, and support. You trusted your Guru Within.

The more you trust your Guru Within, the more messages you will receive. Sometimes, all you can do is listen. The messages may not always make sense to you at first, but you must pay attention to them. They are preparing you for something that will happen later. For instance, sometimes in my treatment room I feel a brief, physical discomfort, seemingly out of nowhere. When I first feel this sensation, I do not understand why I'm feeling it. However, later that day, a client will come in complaining of exactly the same pain I felt earlier. That's how I know my discomfort came from the Guru

Awakening the Guru Within

Within: it was preparing me for the work I would do later.

In those kinds of moments — when your Guru Within sends you an insight before you know what it means — you do not have to act. You simply have to listen to the insight, trusting that your Guru Within will help you understand it later. Other times, however, you *do* have to act on your messages. You have free will to choose to act or not. The messages may reappear until you take action, or they may move onto someone else who is willing to do the work. You cannot know which messages are yours alone and which are universal; you cannot know which messages could happen anytime and which must happen now. That is why you must trust your Guru Within and act when you are guided to do so. Otherwise, you will miss crucial opportunities to move closer to fulfilling your purpose and destiny.

However, reaching this level of trust in your Guru Within will take time. Start from where you are. Small steps lead to bigger steps. At times in our life, the universe gives us just enough light to see the next step. When you take that step, the universe will illuminate the next step as well. You need to trust the universe and your Guru Within enough to take each step. When you cannot tell what is real and what is your ego, pause. Reflect on what you are receiving. If your Guru

Joyce Fennell

Within is preparing you for a big step, its message will start as a whisper and grow louder over time. Eventually, you will no longer be able to ignore the message: you must take the action required.

Be mindful of your destiny and purpose when you choose to act on these messages. Ask yourself: *"What if I do this?* Will my life experience grow? Will be in service to my world? Will I become a brighter light for others? Will I reach my highest, best life?" Then, ask yourself the reverse: *"What if I don't do this?* Will I be unable to move forward in other areas of my life? Who in my life will not get what they need? Will I regret not taking action? Will I get another opportunity like this?"

The takeaway here is to trust the process. Listen to your Guru Within. Trust the information it gives you and, as always, trust yourself. When you trust your Guru Within more, you will begin to hear even bigger, louder messages. Ask for help and clarity when you need it. You will learn to sense the world around you — politics, the environment, people — in a new way. You may even be able to sense others' energies, gauging how they feel from the smallest contact.

Awakening the Guru Within

What is Holding You Back?

In our lives, we may have had to shut down certain parts of ourselves to protect us from danger or perceived danger. Shutting down parts of ourselves can create energy blocks — physically, emotionally, spiritually, even in our souls. Once those dangers pass, the energy blocks remain, whether we recognize them or not. Moving through these energy blocks is crucial to Awakening. Working through your energy blocks will Awaken parts of yourself that you have not yet been able to access, until now. Awakening these parts will help you reach the all-knowing parts of yourself, your soul: The Guru Within.

What is holding you back from breaking those energy blocks? The answer is simple: you. Blaming others for your current situation will not free you. As you move into the next phase of life, you must start examining yourself. Old ideas, thoughts, or conditioning may be holding you back. You may fear the unknown; you may even fear success. Being extraordinary, instead of ordinary, can feel uncomfortable. We may have been conditioned to feel small and regard others' feelings above our own. On some level, these feelings teach us empathy: they encourage us to help the less fortunate and take care of

Joyce Fennell

loved ones who need us. Too often, however, we take this message too far, forsaking ourselves and our own needs in the process. I'm here to say, "Stop it!" Put yourself back into the equation. You are no good to anyone unless you are first good to yourself. We are all born to be not just ordinary, but extraordinary in some part of our lives. We must accept and embrace the greatness of our potential.

In my work as a massage therapist, energy healer, light worker, intuitive, and empath, I have had the opportunity to help my clients move their energy blocks. My work is unique: I use my own version of different practices and modalities, bringing in a mix of physical massage and energy healing along with your intuition, empathy, and spirituality. Through my life's work — both in my practice and in this book — my intention is to help my clients improve their lives. I hope your life will improve because of the information in this book, as well as the intention with which it was written. From my experience, I know you cannot move forward until you remove the energy blocks that stand in your way. You must release the blocks in your physical, spiritual, and emotional bodies so that you can access the metaphysical.

To do this, you must first feel your physical body. You must notice what you are feeling and where you

Awakening the Guru Within

are feeling it. Find a comfortable position where you will not be disturbed — reclining in an armchair, perhaps, or lying on a bed. Then, be still and quiet. Breathe deeply into your solar plexus. Think of the breaths as cleansing and purifying. With each breath, relax every part of your physical body. Relax your head, neck, arms, shoulders, diaphragm, and upper chest; relax your ribs, solar plexus, lower back, pelvis, legs, and feet. Breathe and feel the lightness. Take a few more deep, cleansing breaths. Enjoy this unwinding of your skeletal and muscular systems. If you feel lingering tension in any part of your body, breathe into it and focus on that area. Ask again to relax and release tension.

Allow yourself to feel your physical body's lightness. Keep breathing deeply for a few more breaths. When you're ready, begin breathing normally again. Now, ask all your organs to relax as well. Begin at the top of your head: ask your brain to release any and all tension, stress, and toxic material. Relax and release it now. Do the same with your eyes, your ears and your jaw. Release your thyroid gland in your throat; move into your heart, lungs, esophagus, and stomach. Then, move into your kidneys, liver, gallbladder, spleen, and pancreas. Release now. Move into your small and large intestines, your bladder, and your reproductive organs. Release any and all toxic materials that remain in these parts of your body. Breathe into this experience. Imagine that on each exhale, you are releasing any and all energy that does not serve your highest good.

Imagine all of your body's systems, from circulatory, respiratory, reproductive, and skeletal to muscular and endocrine. Release any lingering stress, tension, and toxic material from them now. Take in a few cleansing breaths. Now, we will clean up and clear your systems out. When you are ready, imagine a golden-white ball of light in your third eye chakra, in the center of your forehead. See and feel its smooth surface, like metal or glass, moving in a circular motion. Ask this golden-white ball to move freely through your body, gathering any and all toxic particles that you have released. Let the ball move freely around your head, neck, and throat; let it move down your upper chest, shoulders, and upper back. The ball will gather all the toxic material you have already released.

Visualize the golden-white ball splitting into two balls at your heart chakra center: one ball moves down your left arm and one moves down your right, each ending in your hands. Feel the sensation in the palm of your hands. Visualize the balls moving back up your arms and into your upper chest, and down through

Awakening the Guru Within

your esophagus, lungs, diaphragm, stomach, intestines, solar plexus, middle and lower back, and reproductive organs. The balls continue down each of your legs, all the way to the soles of your feet. Feel the sensation there now. Breathe in and out, again and again, and ask the golden-white balls to release into Mother Earth. With them, they carry the toxic energies you have released. Affirm aloud: "I release you into the Mother because I no longer need to carry you. I am grateful for all you have brought into my life. I release you now so that I may receive new energies, light and healing. Amen."

Once you have released those energies into Mother Earth, begin to fill yourself with healing light. When you are ready, take a few, cleansing breaths. Imagine a golden light coming down from the Heavens, towards the top of your head — your crown chakra. Welcome this light of love and healing. Now, imagine this light entering the top of your head, bathing each and every part of your being with its vibrancy and healing. Feel a sense of calm wash over you. Be present with the energies coming into your physical, emotional, and spiritual bodies. Let this bathe each and every cell organ and body system with this radiant healing light. Stay in this radiant light for as long as you like. Thank the divine universal energies for sending this light to fill and heal your mind, body, and spirit. Go out into your life with a new sense of being, as if you have been reborn. Begin noticing any and all changes in your life, physically, emotionally, and even spiritually.

Work with this exercise whenever you want or need to. You may want to record yourself reading this process and listen to the recording as you do it, if that would help. You could also ask a friend to read this exercise aloud, or you and a friend could do this exercise together. Do whatever you need to do to cleanse your body and feel your energies shift. Once you have removed the energy blocks that have been holding you back, you will become an open channel for goodness and light.

Imagine yourself as an empty glass that can be filled with whatever you choose. Through this exercise, we filled your glass with water: the clearest, purest, most natural substance on our planet. Choose to fill your glass with energies that are authentic to your best self, that are part of you already, just as water is already a part of you. Be mindful of what you let into your body, on both physical and energetic levels. Your body makes it possible for your soul, your spirit, to live on this earth. Only in a physical form can you experience all humanity has to offer: love, happiness, peace, joy, gratitude, and so much more.

Awakening the Guru Within

Your purpose and destiny on this earth may be bigger than you could have ever imagined. We do not know what our futures hold. If we did, we could sabotage ourselves, saying, "I could never do that." Remember instead that you have a lifetime of unfolding and enlightenment to experience. Do your best to enjoy this process. Be present and mindful, and be grateful for all you receive on your mystical, magnificent journey every day. You are powerful beyond measure, and you have the power to Awaken to your purpose and achieve your destiny, one step at a time.

Your time is *now*.

Epilogue

We are all spiritual beings, having a human experience. The next form you take may not be human. I am sure, once you reach that level, you will have an amazing experience. However, we must not squander our time in human bodies. Embrace your physical humanity. See, hear, smell, taste, and touch the human world. Enjoy life's goodness. Enjoy the feeling of everything, from babies' soft skin to sand on your feet. Admire the waters, majestic trees, and mountains around you. Take in every part of your human life as part of your spiritual experience.

Be in gratitude for this life. Affirm out loud:

"*I am* one with the higher powers, divine universal energies, and nature."

"*I am* the co-creator of my life. I have the power to live my purpose and destiny. It is my birthright."

"*I am* ready to receive all that I have come here to receive."

"*I am* ready to do the work that I am here to do."

"*I am* ready to be in service to the greater good."

"*I am* an open vessel. Please fill me with all I need to know, so that I may go out and do the work I am here to do and live the life I am here to live."

"*Allow me* do this work with divine guidance and a sense of purpose, for the greater good of all humanity and the world."

"*I am* in gratitude for all my life experiences, past, present, and future."

Feel blessed, for you are blessed. Remember this verse as you move forward into the rest of your life.

I leave you with this final message:

As you stand on the edge of your personal greatness,

Pause, turn around, and witness how far you have come.

Be in gratitude for your journey and how far it has brought you.

As you stand on the edge of your personal greatness,

Take a small step or a giant leap.

Allow yourself to fall freely, into whatever comes next.

Peace.

Joyce Fennell

Recommended Reading

Ask and it is Given: Learning to Manifest Your Desires, Esther Hicks and Jerry Hicks, 2004

Earth Angels, Doreen Virtue, 2002

The Healing Code: 6 Minutes to Heal the Source of Your Health, Success or Relationship Issue, Alexander Loyd, 2013

The Four Agreements: A Practical Guide to Personal Freedom, Don Miguel Ruiz, 1997

The Book of Awakening: Having the Life You Want by Being Present to the Life You Have, Mark Nepo, 2000

Dodging Energy Vampires: An Empath's Guide to Evading Relationships That Drain You and Restoring Your Health and Power, Christiane Northrup, 2018

Joyce Fennell

The Power of Now: A Guide to Spiritual Enlightenment, Eckhart Tolle, 2004

The Energy Bus: 10 Rules to Fuel Your Life, Work and Team with Positive Energy, Jon Gordon, 2007

Notes

Chapter 1

Jean Houston, "Gee, you are you!"

Chapter 3

Gladwell, Malcolm, *Outliers: The Story of Success*, 2008

Made in the USA
Lexington, KY
28 December 2018